10-00

7 INGREDIENTS STUDENT Cookbook

4 INGREDIENTS Student Cookbook

200 $\left(\dfrac{\text{FAST+EASY}}{\text{recipes}}\right)$ x 4 ingredients

hamlyn

An Hachette UK Company
www.hachette.co.uk

First published in Great Britain in 2010
by Hamlyn, a division of Octopus Publishing
Group Ltd
Endeavour House
189 Shaftesbury Avenue
London
WC2H 8JY
www.octopusbooks.co.uk

ISBN: 978-0-600-62110-2

A CIP catalogue record for this book is
available from the British Library

Printed and bound in China

10 9 8 7 6 5 4 3 2

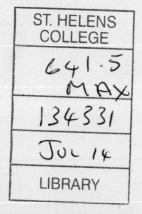
Notes

This book includes dishes made with nuts and
nut derivatives. It is advisable for those
with known allergic reactions to nuts and nut
derivatives and those who may be potentially
vulnerable to these allergies, such as
pregnant and nursing mothers, invalids, the
elderly, babies and children, to avoid dishes
made with nuts and nut oils. It is also
prudent to check the labels of preprepared
ingredients for the possible inclusion of nut
derivatives.

The Department of Health advises that eggs
should not be consumed raw. This book contains
some dishes made with raw or lightly cooked
eggs. It is prudent for more vulnerable people
such as pregnant and nursing mothers,
invalids, the elderly, babies and young
children to avoid uncooked or lightly cooked
dishes made with eggs.

Meat and poultry should be cooked thoroughly.
To test if poultry is cooked, pierce the flesh
through the thickest part with a skewer or
fork - the juices should run clear, never pink
or red.

Both metric and imperial measurements are
given for the recipes. Use one set of measures
only, not a mixture of both.

Ovens should be preheated to the specified
temperature. If using a fan-assisted oven,
follow the manufacturer's instructions for
adjusting the time and temperature. Grills
should also be preheated.

CONTENTS

Introduction 6

Essentials 14

Breakfasts & brunches 18

Classic comforts 40

Pasta & pizza 70

Vegetarian dishes 100

Asian dishes 122

Meals for mates 140

Healthy fixes 160

TV dinners & snacks 180

Desserts & sweet treats 202

Cakes & bakes 228

Index 250

Acknowledgements 256

INTRODUCTION

NO CASH, NO CLUE

For most of us student life offers a range of challenges, not the least of which are having to live away from home for the first time and having to cook for ourselves. Although students have a reputation for eating nothing but instant noodles and cold baked beans, most do appreciate good food and want to eat healthily. But basic cooking facilities and a tight budget make this far from easy, especially when they are combined with the fact that most students don't have much of a clue about what and how to cook.

The solution is to create a repertoire of quick, easy, adaptable dishes, that are not only cheap and tasty but that also require little shopping and preparation. And this is where this book comes in. Adopting the simple four-ingredient formula will allow you to master some basic recipes in record time and learn to appreciate that cooking for yourself is a satisfying and empowering process. Properly prepared food will not only keep your body together, but your soul too. Your entire student experience will pass much more smoothly if you are happy with what you are eating: your life will be more secure and better organized. Don't forget, too, the popularity value of food. Students are always hungry, so if you can put together a simple meal, cook a stack of pancakes or even just bake a cake, you will create a friendly group atmosphere and make new friends.

How four-ingredient cooking works

The recipes in this book have been chosen not only for their simplicity and great flavours, but also because they use just four or fewer main ingredients together with a limited number of specified extras. This will make your life easier in three ways. First, because the recipes are straightforward there is less fiddly preparation, which will save you time. Second, you will find that shopping is simpler. How long do you really want to wander around a supermarket searching for something to cook? And third, it will save money. The four-ingredient approach will mean that you don't have cupboards full of half-used packets of strange ingredients, left over from previous meals, that you will never use again.

Start by stocking up on the storecupboard essentials listed on pages 14—17. These are ingredients — flour, dried herbs, garlic, oil and butter, for example — that you will use frequently. Make sure that you have at least some of them at all times so you know you are just four ingredients away from any of the great recipes in this book.

Next, choose a recipe that suits the time you have to cook, your energy levels and your mood. Cooking and preparation times are noted at the top of each recipe to help you plan your time effectively. The essential ingredients — those you will have in your storecupboard — are listed on the right of the page. On the left are the four or fewer extra ingredients that you will need to go and buy to complete the dish. When you are ready to cook read the recipe through and then follow the simple steps for a quick and delicious meal.

Etiquette in a shared kitchen

* Start a kitty for food if you are eating together and make sure that everyone contributes a set amount each week.

* Prepare a shopping list together once a week and then take it in turns to do the shopping.

* If you have a kitty decide what will be included. You need to set a few rules about who will foot the bill for luxury items, such as alcohol and biscuits.

* If you are eating together take it in turns to cook.

* Make it a rule that no dirty dishes are left at the end of the day, even if you have to draw up a rota to achieve this.

GREAT GRUB ON A SHOE STRING

Budgeting for food is like budgeting for anything else: work out how much you've got to spend each week and don't spend more, or you'll be living on toast for the last few weeks of term.

One of the best ways to eat cheaply is to avoid costly processed foods. Instead, buy basic ingredients, such as vegetables, rice, pasta, fish and chicken, and build your meals around these. You should also try to avoid waste and not spend money on food you don't eat and that has to be thrown away. Buy food that lasts — get packets of dried herbs instead of fresh, for example, so there's no waste if you use only a small amount immediately. If you have a freezer, freeze the leftovers for another day.

Try to use the oven economically to minimize gas or electricity bills. If you are cooking a casserole, for instance, bake some potatoes and other vegetables at the same time to serve with it.

Be organized

Planning ahead is an important part of keeping yourself fed. Plan your meals at the start of the week so you need to go shopping only once a week. When you get into the habit of doing this the ingredients for each meal will be waiting when you need them.

It's also a good idea to plan your menus so that you can use up leftover ingredients from earlier meals. For example, cook Quick Sausage and Bean Casserole (see page 50) at the start of the week, then Sausage and Sweet Potato Hash (see page 60) later in the week to use up the rest of the sausages.

Keep a few basics — pasta and tinned tomatoes, for example — in your cupboard for quick meals when you've had no time to shop or when friends turn up unexpectedly. Even better, cook in batches and freeze some portions for instant meals when you need them. This will also save you time and money. Soups freeze well — try Curried Carrot and Lentil Soup (see page 46) — as do baked dishes, such as Shepherd's Pie (see page 52).

Canny shopping

Cooking on a budget is always a challenge, but there are plenty of things you can do to make your money go further.

Buy in bulk to get the best prices. Come to an arrangement with some friends to buy the largest bags of pasta and pulses you can find, then share them out. Make time to shop around and compare prices in the nearest supermarket, your local shops and on market stalls to see which is cheapest. Remember that own-brand goods are almost always cheaper than products with a well-known brand name.

Stick to buying fruit and vegetables that are in season. Not only will they be better value than exotic produce flown in from abroad but you will be reducing your food miles.

Healthy and happy

* Base your meals on starchy carbohydrates, such as pasta, potatoes, rice, bread and couscous. They will fill you up and give you energy.

* Aim to eat at least five portions of fruit and vegetables each day, whether they are fresh, frozen, tinned, dried or juiced. Eat an apple as a snack, keep a bag of peas in the freezer and add them to recipes, and drink a glass of fruit or vegetable juice. Each of these counts as a 'portion'.

* Make sure you get some protein every day. Good-value sources include pulses (baked beans count here), chicken, tinned fish, liver and eggs.

* Drink a glass of milk each day; it's full of calcium and vitamins.

Finally, don't even think about spending precious cash on a supermarket's 'special offer' unless it is something you will actually use. Three tins of pilchards in mustard sauce for the price of two is good value only if you are going to eat them.

STUDENT SURVIVAL TIPS

Piles of dirty saucepans in the sink and a piece of mouldy cheese in the refrigerator may make it feel like a student house, but it's worth observing a few simple hygiene rules to make sure that you and your housemates survive safely to the end of term.

Always wash your hands before you prepare food, and wash dishcloths and tea towels regularly — they are breeding grounds for bacteria. Wash up after every meal so that nasty bugs cannot breed on the dirty dishes.

Check the use-by dates on fresh foods, especially meat and fish, and throw away anything that is out of date. Throw away any mouldy food that you find in the refrigerator — don't just cut off the furry bit because there may be toxins in the rest of the food. If you drop food on the floor, wash it before you eat it. If it is toast that has fallen butter side down, forget the 10-second rule and bin it.

Put leftover cooked food in the refrigerator as soon as it is cool. Don't eat food that has been left at room temperature overnight — it's not worth the risk — and if you are reheating cooked food make sure it is piping hot right the way through.

Handling meat and poultry

* Thoroughly wash your hands, chopping boards and knives immediately after touching raw meat or poultry.

* Store raw meat and poultry in the refrigerator. Make sure it is properly wrapped and cannot touch or drip on other foods.

* Cook poultry and pork thoroughly. To test them insert a sharp knife or skewer into the thickest part of the meat — the juices should run clear, with no hint of pinkness.

* Reheat cooked meat and poultry thoroughly. It must be piping hot right through to the middle.

Essential equipment

No one is suggesting that you fill your cupboards with egg slicers, melon ballers or gadgets for removing stones from olives, but there are several bits of equipment that you will need.

Investing in a few good-quality items of kitchen equipment will be well worth the time and effort, but remember that you can still save money in this area. Get the cheapest plates, bowls and mugs you can find — they're almost certain to get broken sooner or later — and shop around for cheap cutlery. It's likely that everyone's cutlery will end up in the same drawer anyway, and a cheap spoon works just as well as an expensive one.

Saucepans Ideally, buy two or three of different sizes, avoiding those with a nonstick coating, which will get ruined. You will need a large pan for cooking pasta and rice, and if you get one with metal handles it can go in the oven too.

Frying pan Buy a large, good-quality pan, which will last.
Sharp knife A good-quality kitchen knife will give you years of service. A knife with a 20 cm (8 inch) blade is most versatile.
Chopping board You will need a board to protect the work surfaces in the kitchen — and make sure you get your deposit back at the end of the year.
Colander You can use this for draining pasta, rice, potatoes and vegetables and for washing salad.
Measuring jug You will be surprised how often you use a measuring jug, especially as you begin to experiment with recipes. Anyway, what else will you serve gravy or custard in?
Wooden spoon You will need a wooden spoon when you try baking biscuits and cakes, but you can also use it for stirring food in saucepans to avoid scratching them.
Potato masher Use it to make smooth mashed potatoes, of course, but also for swede, parsnip and other delicious vegetable mashes.
Tin opener Not all tins have ring pulls.

ESSENTIALS

1 / Plain flour

You will need plain flour for sauces, pastry and baking. Start with a small bag and see how much you use. It isn't expensive, and you could share it with others in your accommodation.

2 / Self-raising flour

You will need self-raising flour if you intend to do a lot of baking because (unlike plain flour) it contains a raising agent. Again, start with a small bag and see how much you use.

3 / Sugar, granulated or caster

Caster sugar can be used in any recipe that calls for granulated sugar. It is finer than granulated sugar, which means that you can use it in tea, coffee and hot chocolate, but it is slightly more expensive than granulated. However, if you only want to buy one type and intend to do some baking you should buy caster sugar. Demerara sugar can be used for coffee and in some puddings.

4 / Stock cubes

Ideally, you should have vegetable, chicken, beef, lamb and fish stock cubes (or granules) to reconstitute in boiling water whenever stock is called for in a recipe. It wouldn't be the end of the world if you used vegetable stock cubes for everything because they have quite a mild flavour. Most stock cubes are quite salty, so don't add extra salt until you've tasted your cooking.

5 / Salt and pepper

Sea salt and freshly ground black pepper are the best types to use, but see what you can afford. They are essential ingredients for seasoning nearly all savoury dishes, but remember to add them sparingly and taste the recipe after each addition.

6 / Dried herbs

Dried herbs of various kinds are used in many sauces and casseroles. The main ones you will need are bay leaves, parsley, thyme, marjoram, sage and mint, but you may need others, such as oregano and coriander leaves. Buy them as you need them and store them in a cool, dark place. They are available in small jars. If you prefer to use fresh herbs, you should use twice the quantity given for the dried equivalent. Similarly, if you use dried herbs instead of fresh you should halve the quantity because dried herbs have a more intense flavour.

7 / Dried spices

Ground coriander seeds, cumin, paprika, cayenne pepper, caraway, cinnamon, nutmeg and turmeric are used in many recipes and are worth buying. Like dried herbs, they are available in small jars, which should be kept in a cool, dark cupboard. It is not worth buying large quantities of ingredients that you will use only rarely because they lose their colour and flavour if they are kept for too long.

8 / Chilli powder and/or dried chilli flakes

These are essential for adding heat to dishes. They are available hot or medium, as you prefer. Use them sparingly and taste after each addition.

9 / Olive oil

It is worth buying olive oil, which is great for frying and for drizzling over pizzas and salads. It can also be combined with balsamic vinegar to make a dressing for salads, or to have with bread. It varies widely in price according to how pure it is, so buy what suits your budget and start with a small bottle and see how much you use.

10 / Vegetable oil or sunflower oil

Both these oils are less expensive than olive oil and can be used for shallow-frying, such as eggs, or deep-frying, such as chips, as well as roasting. Use whichever you prefer. If you like to drizzle oil over salads and pasta you will need to use olive oil.

11 / Tomato purée

Use tomato purée to add flavour to sauces, casseroles and so on. It is available in tubes and jars and keeps for a while in the refrigerator once opened.

12 / Medium curry paste

You will need curry paste for curries or curried dishes. Buy a small jar to start with and store it in the refrigerator once opened. You could use curry powder instead, which keeps longer, but check the packaging for how much to use. There are also mild and hot types, so experiment with the different strengths.

13 / Sweet chilli sauce

This makes a great dip for Chinese dishes and can be used as an accompaniment to burgers, deep-fried fish and so on.

14 / Soy sauce

An essential addition to most Chinese dishes, soy sauce is available in light and dark varieties. Buy a small jar of light soy sauce to start with. It has a salty flavour so use sparingly.

15 / Balsamic vinegar

The intense flavour is great on grilled goods and on salads. It can be expensive so buy according to your budget.

16 / Semi-skimmed milk

Essential for midnight bowls of cereal, you can also use milk in sauces. It's available in plastic bottles in a wide range of sizes, up to about 3.6 litres (6 pints), but don't buy more than you will use in a day or two and always keep it in the refrigerator. You can also get skimmed and full-fat milk if you prefer.

17 / Margarine

You can use margarine for sandwiches, frying, making sauces and baking. Check the label to make sure that it is suitable for the recipe you are making, because some aren't good for frying, while others aren't good in cakes. It's mostly available in plastic tubs in 250 g (8 oz) and 500 g (1 lb) weights. Keep it in the refrigerator.

18 / Butter

Although it's more expensive than margarine, butter has a superior flavour, and can be used instead of margarine in all recipes, although the 'spreadable' types can be more easily spread on bread and toast. You can use butter in sauces and for baking, when it should taken from the refrigerator and left to come to room temperature before use.

19 / 6 eggs

Buy free-range eggs if you can afford them. They are a perfect storecupboard stand-by, and you can use them on their own for boiled, scrambled, poached and fried eggs and to make frittatas and omelettes. You will also need eggs if you plan to do any baking, but check the recipe before you begin to make sure that you have enough in stock.

20 / Bulb of garlic

Garlic, finely sliced or crushed, is used as a flavouring in all kinds of dishes, from Italian to Chinese and from French to Thai. Buy a bulb and use one clove at a time.

21 / Lemon juice

This adds flavour and gloss to sauces as well as enhancing the flavour of casseroles and other meat dishes. You can buy lemon juice in plastic containers, which makes it easier to measure than squeezing it from the fruit.

BREAKFASTS & BRUNCHES

BOILED EGGS WITH MUSTARD SOLDIERS

Serves 2
Preparation time 5 minutes
Cooking time 5 minutes

1 teaspoon **wholegrain or ordinary mustard**, to taste

2 thick slices of **white bread**

Essentials
25 g (1 oz) butter, softened
2 large eggs
pepper

Beat together the mustard, butter and pepper in a small bowl.

Cook the eggs in a saucepan of boiling water for 4—5 minutes until softly set.

Meanwhile, toast the bread, then butter one side with the mustard butter and cut into fingers. Serve the eggs with the mustard soldiers.

FRENCH TOAST

Serves 2
Preparation time 5 minutes
Cooking time about 6 minutes

2 slices of **fruit bread**

Essentials
1 egg
1 tablespoon milk
15 g (½ oz) butter
1 tablespoon vegetable oil
1 tablespoon sugar
pinch of ground cinnamon
  (optional)

Cut the fruit bread into strips or triangles with a knife or use a biscuit cutter to cut out other shapes.

Put the egg and milk in a shallow bowl and beat together lightly.

Heat the butter and oil in a frying pan. Dip a few pieces of bread in the egg mixture, turning to cover. Lift the bread from the egg mixture, letting the extra drain back into the bowl.

Add the bread to the frying pan and cook, turning once, for 2—3 minutes or until golden. Transfer the cooked bread to kitchen paper to drain and repeat with the remaining bread and egg mixture.

Sprinkle with the sugar and cinnamon (if used).

If liked, serve with a few satsuma or orange segments.

BACON & EGGS

Serves 2
Preparation time 5 minutes
Cooking time 9—11 minutes

4 ripe **tomatoes**
2 tablespoons chopped **fresh basil**
2 slices of **bacon**
1 tablespoon **vinegar**

Essentials
3 tablespoons olive oil
4 large eggs
salt and pepper

Halve the tomatoes and arrange them, cut side up, on a grill pan. Mix the basil with 2 tablespoons of the oil and drizzle over the cut tomatoes. Season well with salt and pepper. Cook under a preheated grill for about 6—7 minutes, until softened. Remove and keep warm.

Meanwhile, heat the remaining oil in a frying pan and fry the bacon until crisp. Drain on kitchen paper and keep warm.

Add the vinegar to a pan of gently simmering water and poach the eggs for 3—4 minutes or until just set.

If liked, serve on hot buttered toasted muffins with the bacon and grilled tomatoes.

EGGS BENEDICT

Serves 2
Preparation time 15 minutes
Cooking time 15 minutes

4 thick slices of **cooked ham**

1 tablespoon **single cream**

1 tablespoon **vinegar**

2 **muffins** or slices of **brioche**

Essentials
4 eggs
15 g (½ oz) butter

Hollandaise sauce
3 egg yolks
125 g (4 oz) butter,
  softened
large pinch of salt
pinch of cayenne pepper
1 teaspoon lemon juice

Cook the ham under a preheated grill for 2—3 minutes on each side.
Transfer to an ovenproof dish and keep warm.

Make the sauce. Beat together the egg yolks and 1 tablespoon water
in a heatproof bowl set above a saucepan of simmering water until
the mixture is pale. Gradually add the butter, a little at a time,
and continue beating until the mixture thickens. Add the salt,
cayenne pepper and lemon juice. Stir in the cream. Remove from the
heat and keep warm. Add the vinegar to a pan of gently simmering
water and poach the eggs for 3—4 minutes or until just set.

Meanwhile, split and toast the muffins or brioche slices and
spread them with the butter. Arrange them on warm plates. Place a
slice of ham on each muffin half and top with a poached egg. Spoon
a little of the sauce over each egg.

Garnish with another pinch of cayenne pepper and some snipped
chives, if liked, and serve at once.

ALL-IN-ONE VEGGIE BREAKFAST

Serves 2
Preparation time 10 minutes
Cooking time 35 minutes

250 g (8 oz) **cooked potatoes**, cubed

125 g (4 oz) **button mushrooms**, trimmed

6 **cherry tomatoes**

Essentials
2 tablespoons olive oil
2 eggs
salt and pepper

Spread the potato cubes out in a roasting tin. Drizzle over half the oil and season with salt and pepper. Bake in a preheated oven, 220°C (425°F), Gas Mark 7, for 10 minutes.

Stir the potato cubes well, add the mushrooms and bake for 10 minutes. Add the tomatoes and bake for a further 10 minutes.

Make 2 hollows between the vegetables and carefully break an egg into each hollow. Bake for 3—4 minutes until the eggs are set.

Serve straight from the tin with buttered toast, if liked.

MIXED MUSHROOMS ON TOAST

Serves 2
Preparation time 10 minutes
Cooking time 5 minutes

375 g (12 oz) **mixed mushrooms**, such as flat, button, oyster, shiitake, trimmed and sliced

2 tablespoons chopped **fresh parsley**

2 slices of **bread**

Essentials
15 g (½ oz) butter
1–2 tablespoons olive oil, plus extra to serve
1 garlic clove, crushed
1 tablespoon lemon juice
salt and pepper

Melt the butter with the oil in a large frying pan. As soon as the butter stops foaming, add the mushrooms and garlic. Season with salt and pepper and cook over a medium heat, stirring, for 4–5 minutes until tender. Scatter over the parsley and a little lemon juice.

Meanwhile, toast the bread and arrange on serving plates. Top the toast with equal quantities of the mushrooms and drizzle over a little more oil and lemon juice.

Scatter with Parmesan shavings, if liked, and serve immediately.

SCRAMBLED EGGS WITH GOATS' CHEESE & HERBS

Serves 2
Preparation time 10 minutes
Cooking time 5 minutes

200 g (7 oz) soft **goats' cheese**
2 teaspoons finely snipped
fresh chives

2-4 slices of hot buttered **toast**

Essentials
25 g (1 oz) butter
6 large eggs
2 tablespoons milk
salt and pepper

Melt the butter in a saucepan over a gentle heat until foaming.

Put the eggs in a bowl and mix well with a fork. Add the milk and season with salt and pepper.

Pour the eggs into the foaming butter and cook, stirring constantly with a wooden spoon, scraping the bottom of the pan and bringing the eggs from the outside to the centre. The eggs are done when they form soft, creamy curds and are barely set.

Remove the pan from the heat and stir in the goats' cheese and chives. Pile on to the hot toast on warm serving plates and serve immediately.

PESTO SCRAMBLED EGGS

Serves 2
Preparation time 5 minutes
Cooking time 5 minutes

50 ml (2 fl oz) **single cream**

2 slices of **granary bread**, toasted

2 tablespoons ready-made **pesto**

Essentials
6 eggs
15 g (½ oz) butter
salt and pepper

Beat together the eggs, cream and a little salt and pepper in a bowl. Melt the butter in a large, nonstick frying pan, add the egg mixture and stir over a low heat with a wooden spoon until cooked to your liking.

Put a slice of toast on each warm serving plate. Spoon half the scrambled eggs on to each slice of toast, make a small indentation in the centre and add a tablespoonful of pesto. Serve immediately.

CHEESE & TOMATO OMELETTE

Serves 2
Preparation time 5 minutes
Cooking time 12 minutes

25 g (1 oz) grated **Cheddar cheese**

50 g (2 oz) halved **cherry tomatoes**

Essentials
6 eggs
2 tablespoons milk
25 g (1 oz) butter
salt and pepper

Beat together the eggs, milk and a little salt and pepper in a large bowl.

Melt half the butter in an omelette pan. As soon as it stops foaming, swirl in half the egg mixture and cook over a medium heat, forking over the omelette so that it cooks evenly. As soon as it is set on the underside but is still a little runny in the centre, scatter half the cheese and half the cherry tomatoes over one half of the omelette.

Carefully slide the omelette on to a warm serving plate, folding it in half as you go. Keep warm in a moderate oven while you repeat with the remaining ingredients. Serve immediately.

POTATO RÖSTI WITH FRAZZLED EGGS

Serves 2
Preparation time 15 minutes
Cooking time 15 minutes

375 g (12 oz) **potatoes**

1/2 **onion**, thinly sliced

1 teaspoon chopped **fresh rosemary**

Essentials
2 tablespoons olive oil
2 large eggs
salt and pepper

Coarsely grate the potatoes with a box grater. Wrap them in a clean tea towel and squeeze out the excess liquid over the sink. Transfer to a bowl and stir in the onion and rosemary. Season to taste with salt and pepper.

Heat half the oil in a large frying pan. Divide the potato mixture in half and spoon into 2 mounds, each about 12 cm (5 inches) across, in the pan, pressing it down to form patties. Cook over a medium heat for 5 minutes on each side, transfer to warm serving plates and keep warm in a moderate oven.

Heat the remaining oil in the frying pan for about 1 minute until very hot, add the eggs and fry until the whites are bubbly and the yolks are cooked as you like. Serve the eggs on top of the rösti.

POTATO & BACON CAKES

Serves 2
Preparation time 15 minutes, plus chilling
Cooking time about 45 minutes

500 g (1 lb) **potatoes**, cut into chunks

6 **spring onions**, sliced

200 g (7 oz) **back bacon**, chopped

1 tablespoon chopped **fresh flat leaf parsley**

Essentials
vegetable oil, for frying
plain flour, for coating
25 g (1 oz) butter
salt and pepper

Cook the potatoes in a large saucepan of lightly salted boiling water for 15—20 minutes until tender. Drain well, return to the pan and mash.

Heat a little oil in a frying pan, add the spring onions and cook for 2—3 minutes, then add the bacon and cook until browned. Add to the mash with the parsley. Season well with salt and pepper. Form the potato mixture into 4 cakes, then cover with clingfilm and chill in the refrigerator until firm.

Lightly coat the cakes in flour. Melt the butter in a nonstick frying pan, add the cakes, in 2 batches if necessary, and cook over a medium heat for 4—5 minutes on each side until browned and heated through.

Serve the cakes hot with baked beans, if liked.

RÖSTI WITH HAM & EGGS

Serves 2
Preparation time 10 minutes
Cooking time 10–12 minutes

500 g (1 lb) waxy **potatoes,**
such as Desiree

2 slices of **smoked ham**

Essentials
25 g (1 oz) butter
2 eggs
salt and pepper

Coarsely grate the potatoes with a box grater. Wrap them in a clean tea towel and squeeze out the excess liquid over the sink. Transfer to a bowl and season to taste with salt and pepper.

Melt the butter in a large, nonstick frying pan. Divide the potato mixture into 4 and form each portion into a pattie about 10 cm (4 inches) across. Add to the pan and cook over a medium heat for 5–6 minutes on each side until lightly golden. Meanwhile, poach or fry the eggs.

Serve the röstis topped with an egg and a slice of smoked ham.

BACON & MAPLE SYRUP PANCAKES

Serves 2
Preparation time 5 minutes
Cooking time 15 minutes

2 teaspoons **baking powder**
4 rashers of **smoked back bacon**
maple syrup, for drizzling

Essentials
150 g (5 oz) plain flour
½ teaspoon salt
1 egg, lightly beaten
200 ml (7 fl oz) milk
15 g (½ oz) butter, melted
vegetable oil, for frying

Sift the flour, baking powder and salt into a bowl. Make a well in the centre and gradually beat in the egg and milk. Continue to beat until the batter is smooth. Stir in the melted butter.

Heat a heavy-based frying pan until hot, brush lightly with oil and spoon in about a quarter of the batter. Cook over a medium heat for 1—2 minutes until bubbles start to appear on the surface. Carefully flip the pancake over and cook for a further 1—2 minutes until browned on the underside. Remove from the pan and keep warm in a preheated oven, 150°C (300°F), Gas Mark 2, while you cook the remainder of the batter; it should make 4 pancakes in total.

Meanwhile, cook the bacon under a preheated high grill for 2 minutes on each side until golden.

Serve the pancakes topped with the bacon and drizzled with maple syrup.

SUGARED FRUIT PANCAKES

Makes 10—12 pancakes
Preparation time 15 minutes
Cooking time 10 minutes

1/2 teaspoon **baking powder**
50 g (2 oz) **blueberries**

Essentials
1 egg
50 ml (2 fl oz) milk
15 g (½ oz) butter,
  softened
50 g (2 oz) plain flour
1 tablespoon caster sugar
vegetable oil, for frying

Separate the egg, putting the yolk in one bowl and the white in another. Mix together the milk and butter and add the mixture to the egg yolk, stirring well.

Put the flour, baking powder and half the sugar in a large bowl. Add the milk mixture and whisk well to make a smooth batter. Stir in the blueberries. Whisk the egg white until it forms firm peaks. Use a large metal spoon to fold the whites into the batter until well mixed.

Heat a little oil in a large frying pan for 1 minute. Add a tablespoon of the batter to one side of the pan so it spreads to make a little cake. Add 2—3 more spoonfuls, depending on the size of the pan, so the pancakes can cook without touching. When the pancakes are golden on the underside (check by lifting with a palette knife or fish slice), flip them over and cook again until golden. Remove the pancakes from the pan and transfer to a serving plate. Keep them warm while you cook the remainder. Sprinkle with the remaining sugar before serving.

SPICED CITRUS CROISSANTS

Serves 2
Preparation time 15 minutes
Cooking time 5 minutes

25 ml (1 fl oz) **soured cream**
1 **orange**
1 small ruby or pink **grapefruit**
2 **croissants**

Essentials
1–2 teaspoons caster sugar

Put the soured cream in a bowl. Grate the rind of half the orange and stir into the cream.

Peel and remove the skin and white membrane from the orange and the grapefruit. Working over a separate bowl to catch the juice, cut between the membranes to separate the segments.

Mix the fruit segments and juice with the sugar in a small saucepan. Heat over a low heat for 1–2 minutes.

Meanwhile, put the croissants on a baking sheet and bake in a preheated oven, 200°C (400°F), Gas Mark 6, for 5 minutes or until thoroughly heated and slightly toasted.

Split the toasted croissants lengthways and spoon the fruit mixture over the bottom halves. Top with a spoonful of the soured cream mixture and replace the top halves. Serve immediately.

CHOCOLATE BANANA CROISSANTS

Serves 2
Preparation time 2 minutes
Cooking time 3 minutes

4 croissants

1 large **banana**, sliced

125 g (4 oz) **milk chocolate**, broken into squares

Use a serrated knife to cut the croissants in half horizontally and put the bases on a baking sheet. Arrange the banana slices on top of the croissant bases. Top with the chocolate squares and cover with the croissant lids.

Bake in a preheated oven, 230°C (450°F), Gas Mark 8, for 3 minutes until the croissants are warmed through and the chocolate has softened. Serve immediately.

CHOCOLATE BRIOCHE SANDWICH

Serves 2
Preparation time 1 minute
Cooking time 3 minutes

4 slices of **brioche**

2 tablespoons ready-made **chocolate spread**

Essentials
25 g (1 oz) butter
4 teaspoons caster sugar

Spread 2 slices of brioche with chocolate spread, then top each with another slice.

Butter the outsides of the chocolate sandwich and sprinkle with the sugar.

Heat a frying pan, griddle or sandwich maker and cook the sandwiches for 3 minutes, turning as needed to cook evenly. Serve immediately.

CHOCOLATE & CINNAMON EGGY BREAD

Serves 2
Preparation time 2 minutes
Cooking time 3 minutes

2 thick slices of **bread**, cut in half

2 teaspoons **cocoa powder**

Essentials
2 eggs
15 g (½ oz) butter
2 tablespoons caster sugar
½ teaspoon ground cinnamon
(optional)

Put the eggs in a shallow bowl and beat them lightly. Press the bread into the egg, turning to coat well.

Melt the butter in a heavy-based pan and add the eggy bread. Cook for 3 minutes, turning as needed to cook evenly.

Mix together the sugar, cocoa powder and cinnamon (if used) on a plate and place the hot eggy bread on top, turning to coat evenly. Serve immediately.

RHUBARB & CUSTARD SMOOTHIE

Makes 400 ml (14 fl oz)
Preparation time 5 minutes

150 g (5 oz) can **rhubarb**

150 g (5 oz) ready-made **custard**

1 teaspoon **icing sugar** (optional)

ice cubes (optional)

Essentials
100 ml (3½ fl oz) milk

Drain the rhubarb and discard the juice.

Put the rhubarb in a food processor or blender with the custard, milk and icing sugar (if used) and process until smooth.

Pour the smoothie into a large glass over ice (if used) and serve immediately.

BANANA & PEANUT BUTTER SMOOTHIE

Makes 400 ml (14 fl oz)
Preparation time 5 minutes

1 ripe **banana**

1 tablespoon **smooth peanut butter**
or 2 teaspoons **tahini paste**

Essentials
300 ml (½ pint) milk

Peel and slice the banana, put it in a freezer container and freeze for at least 2 hours or overnight.

Put the banana, milk and peanut butter or tahini paste in a food processor or blender and process until smooth.

Pour the smoothie into a tall glass and serve immediately.

CLASSIC COMFORTS

LEEK & POTATO SOUP

Serves 2
Preparation time 15 minutes
Cooking time 40 minutes

1 large **leek**, finely sliced
125 g (4 oz) **potatoes**, roughly diced

1 small **onion**, roughly chopped

Essentials
15 g (½ oz) butter
375 ml (13 fl oz) vegetable
  or chicken stock or water
150 ml (¼ pint) milk
salt and pepper

Melt the butter in a large saucepan. Add the leek, potatoes and onion and stir well to coat with the butter. Cover tightly with a piece of greaseproof paper and cook over a gentle heat for about 15 minutes or until the vegetables have softened, stirring frequently to prevent them from browning. Add the stock or water and milk and season to taste with salt and pepper. Bring to the boil, lower the heat and simmer gently for about 20 minutes or until the vegetables are tender.

Purée the mixture in a food processor or blender and process until smooth, then transfer to a clean saucepan. Adjust the seasoning if necessary and heat until very hot. Pour into warm bowls.

Garnish the soup with snipped chives, if liked, and serve immediately.

FEEL-GOOD BROTH

Serves 2
Preparation time 2 minutes
Cooking time about 25 minutes

1 boneless, skinless **chicken breast,** about 150 g (5 oz)

1 slice of **lemon**

1 teaspoon roughly chopped **fresh thyme**

125 g (4 oz) fresh **meat cappelletti** or small **tortellini**

Essentials
450 ml (¾ pint) cold chicken stock
salt and pepper

Put the chicken, stock, lemon slice and thyme in a large saucepan. Bring to a gentle simmer (the water should shiver rather than bubble in the pan). Cover and cook for 15—16 minutes until the chicken is opaque all the way through. Lift the chicken from the liquid with a slotted spoon and transfer to a plate. Remove the lemon slice.

When the chicken is cool enough to handle, shred into large pieces.

Bring the stock to a rapid boil and season to taste with salt and pepper. Add the pasta and cook for 2—3 minutes, adding the shredded chicken for the last minute of the cooking time.

Serve immediately with a generous scattering of grated Parmesan cheese, if liked.

MINTED PEA SOUP

Serves 2
Preparation time 10 minutes
Cooking time 20 minutes

1 small **onion**, finely chopped

1 small **potato**, finely chopped

200 g (7 oz) frozen **peas**

3 tablespoons finely chopped **fresh mint leaves**

Essentials
5 g (¼ oz) butter
500 ml (17 fl oz) vegetable stock
salt and pepper

Melt the butter in a saucepan. Add the onion and potato and cook for 5 minutes. Add the stock and bring to the boil, then reduce heat and simmer gently for 10 minutes or until the potato is tender. Add the peas to the pan and cook for a further 3–4 minutes. Season to taste with salt and pepper, remove from the heat and stir in the mint. Purée in a food processor or blender until smooth. Return to the saucepan to reheat if necessary, then ladle into warm bowls.

Top each bowl with a dollop of crème fraîche, if liked, and serve immediately.

CHUNKY CHICKPEA & PASTA SOUP

Serves 2
Preparation time 5 minutes
Cooking time 35 minutes

1 sprig of **fresh rosemary**, finely chopped

1/2 dried red **chilli**

200 g (7 oz) can **chickpeas**, rinsed and drained

75 g (3 oz) dried **tagliatelle, spaghetti** or **fettuccine**, broken into short lengths

Essentials
1–2 teaspoons olive oil
1 garlic clove, finely chopped
1 tablespoon tomato purée
600 ml (1 pint) vegetable or chicken stock
salt

Heat the oil in a large saucepan over a low heat. Add the garlic, rosemary and chilli and cook, stirring, until the garlic begins to colour. Add the tomato purée and chickpeas and cook, stirring, for 2–3 minutes, then add the stock. Bring to the boil, reduce the heat and simmer gently for 15 minutes. Transfer half the mixture to a food processor or blender and process until smooth. Return it to the pan. Bring to the boil and season to taste with salt.

Add the pasta and cook, stirring frequently, until al dente. Add some boiling water if the soup looks too dry, but the final dish should be thicker than the average soup, yet moister than a classic bowl of pasta.

Leave the soup to stand for 2–3 minutes, and then serve with a scattering of grated Parmesan cheese, if liked.

CURRIED CARROT & LENTIL SOUP

Serves 2
Preparation time 15 minutes
Cooking time 35 minutes

1 small **onion**, chopped

250 g (8 oz) **carrots**, chopped

1 small **potato**, chopped

65 g (2 1/2 oz) **red split lentils**, washed and drained

Essentials
1 tablespoon olive oil
1 small garlic clove, crushed
1—2 teaspoons medium curry paste (to taste)
500 ml (17 fl oz) vegetable stock
salt and pepper

Heat the oil in a saucepan. Add the onion and garlic and cook over a medium heat, stirring frequently, for 5 minutes. Add the carrots, potato and curry paste, stir well and then add the stock and lentils. Season to taste with salt and pepper. Bring to the boil, reduce the heat, cover and simmer gently for 25 minutes.

Transfer to a food processor or blender and process until really smooth. Return to the pan and heat through.

Spoon the soup into warm serving bowls and serve with crusty bread rolls, if liked.

MUSHROOM SOUP

Serves 2
Preparation time 15 minutes, plus soaking
Cooking time 40 minutes

1 tablespoon dried **porcini mushrooms**
1 **onion**, chopped
500 g (1 lb) **flat mushrooms**, trimmed
and chopped

125 ml (4 fl oz) **single cream**, plus extra
to serve

Essentials
40 g (1½ oz) butter
1 garlic clove, crushed
1 tablespoon dried thyme
500 ml (17 fl oz) vegetable
  stock
salt and pepper

Soak the porcini mushrooms in 2 tablespoons boiling
water for 15 minutes. Drain well, reserving the
soaking liquid, then chop the porcini.

Melt half the butter in a saucepan. Add the onions,
garlic and thyme and cook over a low heat, stirring
occasionally, for 10 minutes. Add the remaining
butter and the fresh mushrooms and porcini and
cook over a medium heat, stirring frequently, for
5 minutes, until the mushrooms are softened.

Stir in the stock and the reserved soaking liquid
and bring to the boil, then reduce the heat, cover
and simmer gently for 20 minutes.

Transfer to a food processor or blender and process
until really smooth. Return to the pan, stir in the
cream and heat through without boiling. Spoon the
soup into serving bowls and serve with a swirl of
extra cream.

ROAST ROOT VEGETABLE SOUP

Serves 2
Preparation time 10 minutes
Cooking time 1 hour 5 minutes

2 **carrots**, chopped

1 **parsnip**, chopped

1 **leek**, finely chopped

Essentials
olive oil, for brushing
600 ml (1 pint) vegetable
  stock
½ teaspoon dried thyme
salt and pepper

Put the carrots and parsnip in a roasting tin, brush
lightly with olive oil and season with salt and
pepper. Roast in a preheated oven, 200°C (400°F),
Gas Mark 6, for 1 hour or until the vegetables
are soft.

Meanwhile, 20 minutes before the vegetables have
finished roasting, put the leeks in a large saucepan
with the stock and half the thyme. Cover the pan and
simmer for 20 minutes.

Transfer the roasted root vegetables to a food
processor or blender and process, adding a little of
the stock if the mixture becomes too dry. Transfer
to the stock saucepan and season to taste. Add the
remaining thyme, stir and simmer for 5 minutes to
reheat. Ladle into individual warm bowls and serve.

FRENCH ONION SOUP

Serves 2
Preparation time 15 minutes
Cooking time 1 hour

250 g (8 oz) large **onions**, halved and thinly sliced

75 ml (3 fl oz) **red wine**

2–4 slices of **French bread**

Essentials
15 g (½ oz) butter
1 tablespoon olive oil
1–2 teaspoons sugar
500 ml (17 fl oz) chicken
   stock
1 bay leaf
salt and pepper

Heat the butter and oil in a saucepan. Add the onions and toss in the butter, then fry very gently for 20 minutes, stirring occasionally until soft and just beginning to turn golden around the edges. Stir in the sugar and fry the onions for 20 minutes more, stirring more frequently towards the end of cooking until the onions are caramelized to a rich dark brown.

Add the wine, stock and bay leaf. Season to taste with salt and pepper, then bring to the boil. Cover and simmer for 20 minutes. Taste and adjust the seasoning if needed.

Toast the bread on both sides. Ladle the soup into bowls and top with the toasted bread.

QUICK SAUSAGE & BEAN CASSEROLE

Serves 2
Preparation time 5 minutes
Cooking time 25 minutes

8 cocktail sausages

200 g (7 oz) can chopped tomatoes

200 g (7 oz) can baked beans

100 g (3 1/2 oz) can mixed beans, rinsed and drained

Essentials
1 tablespoon olive oil
1 garlic clove, crushed
½ teaspoon dried thyme
salt and pepper

Heat the oil in a frying pan. Add the sausages and cook until browned all over.

Transfer the sausages to a large saucepan and add all the remaining ingredients. Bring to the boil, then reduce the heat, cover and simmer for 20 minutes. Season to taste with salt and pepper.

Serve the casserole with mashed potatoes, if liked.

BEEF GOULASH

Serves 2
Preparation time 10 minutes
Cooking time 2–2½ hours

375 g (12 oz) **braising steak**, cubed

1 small **onion**, sliced

1 **red pepper**, cored, deseeded and diced

Essentials
1 tablespoon olive oil
1 teaspoon paprika
1–2 teaspoons dried marjoram
½ teaspoon caraway seeds
250 ml (8 fl oz) beef stock
2 tablespoons tomato purée
salt and pepper

Heat the oil in a flameproof casserole. Add the beef, in batches if necessary, and cook over a high heat for 5 minutes until browned all over. Remove from the pan with a slotted spoon.

Add the onion and red pepper to the casserole and cook gently for 10 minutes until softened. Stir in the paprika, marjoram and caraway seeds and cook, stirring, for 1 minute more.

Return the beef to the pan, add the stock and tomato purée. Season to taste with salt and pepper and bring to the boil, stirring. Reduce the heat, cover and simmer gently for 1½–2 hours. You can remove the lid for the final 30 minutes if the sauce needs thickening. Serve with plain boiled rice, if liked.

SHEPHERD'S PIE

Serves 2
Preparation time 20 minutes
Cooking time 1 hour 20 minutes—1 hour 25 minutes

1 small **onion**, finely chopped

250 g (8 oz) **minced lamb**

200 g (7 oz) can **chopped tomatoes**

375 g (12 oz) **potatoes**, cubed

Essentials
1 tablespoon olive oil
1 teaspoon dried thyme
2 tablespoons tomato purée
25 g (1 oz) butter
1—2 tablespoons milk
salt and pepper

Heat the oil in a saucepan. Add the onion and thyme and cook gently for 10 minutes until the onion is soft and golden.

Add the minced lamb and cook over a high heat, breaking up with a wooden spoon, for 5 minutes until browned. Add the tomatoes, tomato purée and salt and pepper to taste. Bring to the boil, reduce the heat, cover and simmer for 30 minutes. Remove the lid and cook for a further 15 minutes until thickened.

Meanwhile, put the potatoes in a large saucepan of lightly salted water and bring to the boil. Reduce the heat and simmer for 15—20 minutes until tender. Drain well and return to the pan. Mash in the butter and milk and season to taste with salt and pepper. Spoon the minced lamb mixture into a 1 litre (1¾ pint) baking dish and carefully spoon the mash over the top, spreading it over the surface of the filling. Bake in a preheated oven, 190°C (375°F), Gas Mark 5, for 20—25 minutes until bubbling and golden.

If liked, add 25 g (1 oz) grated Cheddar cheese to the potatoes with the butter and milk when you mash them and scatter more grated cheese over the top of the potatoes before baking.

EASY FISH PIE

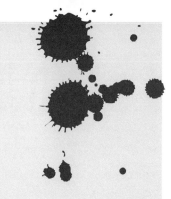

Serves 2
Preparation time 15 minutes
Cooking time 35 minutes

1 small **onion**, finely chopped

150 ml (¼ pint) **double cream**

375 g (12 oz) **white fish** fillets, such as haddock, cod or plaice, cubed

½ small **baguette**, thinly sliced

Essentials
40 g (1½ oz) butter
1 garlic clove, crushed
salt and pepper

Melt half the butter in a saucepan. Add the onion and garlic and cook gently for 10 minutes until soft.

Add the cream and bring to the boil, then reduce the heat and simmer gently for 2 minutes until thickened. Season to taste with salt and pepper. Remove from the heat and stir in the fish. Spoon the mixture into an ovenproof pie dish.

Melt the remaining butter in a small saucepan. Arrange the bread slices over the fish, overlapping them to cover the top, and brush with the melted butter. Bake in a preheated oven, 180°C (350°F), Gas Mark 4, for 15 minutes until the bread is golden. Cover with foil and bake for a further 10 minutes or until the fish is cooked.

TOAD IN THE HOLE

Serves 2
Preparation time 15 minutes
Cooking time 25 minutes

small bunch of **fresh thyme**

250 g (8 oz) extra-lean **pork sausages**

4 rashers of **streaky bacon**

Essentials
25 g (1 oz) plain flour
1 small egg
150 ml (¼ pint) milk
1 tablespoon vegetable oil
salt and pepper

Put the flour and some salt and pepper in a bowl.
Tear the leaves off the thyme stems and add about
1 tablespoon to the bowl along with the egg.
Gradually whisk in the milk until the batter
is smooth and frothy.

Separate the sausages with scissors or a small
knife. Stretch each rasher of bacon by placing it
on a chopping board and running the flat of a knife
along the rasher until it is half as long again.
Wrap bacon around each sausage.

Add the oil to a small roasting tin and add the
bacon-wrapped sausages. Place in a preheated oven,
220°C (425°F), Gas Mark 7, and cook for 5 minutes
until sizzling. Whisk the batter again.

Take the tin out of the oven and quickly pour in
the batter. Put the tin back into the oven and cook
for 15–20 minutes or until the batter is well risen
and golden.

Serve hot with baked beans, if liked.

STEAK WITH HORSERADISH

Serves 2
Preparation time 5 minutes
Cooking time 2—12 minutes

75 ml (3 fl oz) **Greek yogurt**
30 g (1¼ oz) **walnuts,** chopped
25 ml (1 fl oz) **horseradish sauce**
2 **fillet steaks,** each about 125 g (4 oz)

Essentials
1 teaspoon vegetable oil

Make some horseradish cream. Mix together the yogurt, chopped walnuts and horeseradish sauce in a small bowl and set aside.

Heat a ridged griddle pan until smoking and brush the surface with the oil. Add the steaks and cook, turning once only to achieve a decorative ridged effect. The following timing is a rough guide for steaks that are about 2.5 cm (1 inch) thick: blue — cook for 1—2 minutes on each side (soft with no feel of resistance); rare — cook for 2—3 minutes on each side (soft and spongy; may still ooze some red meat juices when pressed); medium rare — cook for 3—4 minutes on each side (a little firmer); medium — cook for 4—5 minutes on each side (firm to the touch); well done — cook for over 5 minutes on each side (solid).

Serve the steaks accompanied by the horseradish cream and with plenty of shredded lettuce leaves, if liked.

PORK STEAKS WITH APPLES

Serves 2
Preparation time 10 minutes
Cooking time about 20 minutes

2 floury **potatoes**, diced

1–2 teaspoons **clear honey**

1 small **green apple**, peeled, cored,
quartered and cut into thick wedges

2 **pork steaks**, each about 200 g (7 oz)

Essentials
1–2 teaspoons dried sage
1 tablespoon olive oil
1–2 teaspoons lemon juice
(to taste)
40 g (1½ oz) butter
1 tablespoon milk
salt and pepper

Cook the potatoes in a saucepan of lightly salted
boiling water for 10 minutes or until tender.
Meanwhile, mix the sage with the oil, lemon juice
and honey and season with salt and pepper. Mix half
the flavoured oil with the apple wedges and brush
the rest over the pork.

Grill the steaks under a preheated medium-hot grill
for 3–4 minutes on each side or until browned and
cooked through. Set aside and keep warm. Drain the
potatoes and mash with a potato masher. Beat in half
the butter and the milk and season to taste with
salt and pepper. Keep warm.

Melt the remaining butter in a frying pan and
quickly fry the apple wedges for 2–3 minutes until
golden and softened.

Serve the pork steaks with the mash, apples and any
pork juices.

FISH 'N' OVEN CHIPS

Serves 2
Preparation time 10 minutes
Cooking time 35—40 minutes

2—3 large **potatoes**, scrubbed

50 g (2 oz) **dried breadcrumbs**

25 g (1 oz) **polenta**

2 **haddock** or **cod** fillets, each about 175 g (6 oz)

Essentials

1 tablespoon olive oil, plus extra for shallow-frying

1—2 teaspoons dried thyme

2 tablespoons plain flour, seasoned with salt and pepper

1 small egg, lightly beaten

salt and pepper

Cut the potatoes into wedges (you should get 8—12 thick wedges from each potato). Toss in the oil, season with salt and pepper and arrange in a layer in a roasting tin. Cook in a preheated oven, 220°C (425°F), Gas Mark 7, for 35—40 minutes, turning once, until evenly browned.

Meanwhile, mix together the breadcrumbs, polenta and thyme in a bowl. Season to taste with salt and pepper. Dust the fish fillets with seasoned flour and then dip into the beaten egg and finally into the breadcrumb mixture, making sure the fish is completely coated.

About 10 minutes before the chips have finished cooking, heat 1 cm (½ inch) oil in a large frying pan, add the fish and cook over a medium heat for 2—3 minutes on each side until the coating is crisp and golden and the fish is cooked through.

Serve the fish with the oven chips and, if liked, some tomato ketchup or mayonnaise.

CHICKEN & RICE BAKE

Serves 2
Preparation time 15 minutes
Cooking time 1 hour

4 boneless, skinless **chicken thighs**, about 375 g (12 oz) in total

4 rashers of **streaky bacon**, rind removed

125 g (4 oz) **long-grain rice**

1 small **onion**, chopped

Essentials
1 tablespoon olive oil
1 garlic clove, crushed
½ teaspoon ground turmeric
250 ml (8 fl oz) hot chicken stock
1 teaspoon dried coriander
1 tablespoon lemon juice
salt and pepper

Wrap each chicken thigh with a bacon rasher and secure in place with a cocktail stick.

Heat the oil in a flameproof casserole, add the chicken and cook over a high heat for 5 minutes until browned all over. Remove with a slotted spoon. Add the rice to the pan and cook over a low heat, stirring, for 1 minute. Add the onion, garlic, turmeric and stock and season to taste with salt and pepper. Arrange the chicken thighs over the rice, pressing them down gently.

Cover with a layer of kitchen foil, then the lid and bake in a preheated oven, 180°C (350°F), Gas Mark 4, for 50 minutes.

Remove from the oven and stir in the coriander and lemon juice. Discard the cocktail sticks and serve.

CHILLI CON CARNE

Serves 2
Preparation time 15 minutes
Cooking time 45 minutes

1 onion, finely chopped

250 g (8 oz) lean minced beef

400 g (13 oz) can chopped tomatoes

400 g (13 oz) can red kidney beans, rinsed and drained

Essentials
2 tablespoons olive oil
3 garlic cloves, finely chopped
½ teaspoon ground cumin
1 tablespoon tomato purée
2 teaspoons chilli powder
200 ml (7 fl oz) beef stock
salt and pepper

Heat the oil in a saucepan. Add the onion and garlic and cook for 5 minutes or until beginning to soften. Add the mince and cumin and cook for a further 5—6 minutes or until browned all over.

Stir in the tomatoes, tomato purée, chilli powder and stock and bring to the boil. Reduce the heat and simmer gently for 30 minutes.

Add the beans and cook for a further 5 minutes. Season to taste with salt and pepper.

If liked, serve with cooked rice.

SAUSAGE & SWEET POTATO HASH

Serves 2
Preparation time 15 minutes
Cooking time 45 minutes

4 **pork sausages**

2 small **onions**, thinly sliced

250 g (8 oz) **sweet potatoes**, cut into small chunks

4 **fresh sage leaves**

Essentials
1½ tablespoons olive oil
½ teaspoon sugar
1 tablespoon balsamic vinegar
salt and pepper

Heat the oil in a frying pan or flameproof casserole and fry the sausages, turning frequently, for about 10 minutes or until browned. Transfer to a plate with a slotted spoon.

Add the onions and sugar to the pan and cook gently, stirring frequently, until lightly browned. Return the sausages to the pan with the sweet potatoes, sage and a little salt and pepper.

Cover the pan with a lid or kitchen foil and cook over a gentle heat for about 25 minutes until the potatoes are tender.

Drizzle with the vinegar and check the seasoning before serving.

TASTY TEATIME PASTIES

Makes 6 pasties
Preparation time 25 minutes, plus chilling
Cooking time 25 minutes

1/2 small **onion**, chopped

175 g (6 oz) lean **lamb**, finely sliced

1 small **potato**, diced

1 teaspoon **Dijon mustard** (optional)

Essentials
375 g (12 oz) plain flour
½ teaspoon salt
175 g (6 oz) butter, cubed
1 tablespoon vegetable oil
300 ml (½ pint) hot lamb
  stock
1 tablespoon dried mint
1 small egg, lightly beaten

Sift the flour and salt into a large mixing bowl and add the butter.
Rub together until the mixture resembles fine breadcrumbs. Add
2–3 tablespoons cold water and mix to form a rough dough. Turn on
to a floured work surface and knead until smooth. Cover with clingfilm
and refrigerate for 30 minutes.

Heat the oil in a frying pan and cook the onion and lamb over a medium
heat, stirring, for 5 minutes or until beginning to brown. Add the
potato, reduce the heat and cook, stirring, for a further 2 minutes
or until browned. Mix the stock with the mustard (if used) and pour
into the pan. Cover with a tight-fitting lid and simmer gently for
15 minutes, stirring occasionally until the potatoes are soft yet
retain their shape and the meat is tender. Stir in the mint and set
aside to cool.

Roll out the pastry to 5 mm (¼ inch) thick and, using a 15 cm (6 inch)
saucer, cut out 6 rounds. Lightly brush the circle edges with water and
put 2 tablespoons of mixture in the centre of each. Fold up to enclose
the filling and pinch and gently twist the edges to seal. Place on a
baking sheet and glaze each one with beaten egg. Bake in a preheated
oven, 200°C (400°F), Gas Mark 6, for 20–25 minutes until golden.

MUSHROOM STROGANOFF

Serves 2
Preparation time 10 minutes
Cooking time 10 minutes

1 small **onion**, thinly sliced

250 g (8 oz) **chestnut mushrooms**, sliced

1 tablespoon **wholegrain mustard**

125 ml (4 fl oz) **crème fraîche**

Essentials
5 g (¼ oz) butter
1 tablespoon olive oil
2 garlic cloves, finely
  chopped
salt and pepper

Melt the butter with the oil in a frying pan. Add the onion and garlic and cook until soft and starting to brown.

Add the mushrooms to the pan and cook until soft and starting to brown. Stir in the mustard and crème fraîche and heat through gently. Season to taste with salt and pepper and serve immediately.

If liked, serve the stroganoff in warm bowls, topped with ready-made croutons and garnished with chopped fresh parsley.

STEAK & ALE CASSEROLE

Serves 2
Preparation time 20 minutes
Cooking time 1½ hours

500 g (1 lb) **braising steak,** cut into chunks
1 **onion,** chopped
200 ml (1 fl oz) **strong ale**
1 tablespoon **black treacle**

Essentials
1 tablespoon plain flour
15 g (½ oz) butter
1 tablespoon vegetable oil
2 teaspoons dried thyme
150 ml (¼ pint) beef stock
salt and pepper

Season the flour with salt and pepper and coat the beef with the flour. Melt the butter with the oil in a large, flameproof casserole. Fry the beef, in batches if necessary, until deep brown. Transfer the meat to a plate with a slotted spoon.

Add the onion and fry gently for 5 minutes. Return the beef to the pan and add the thyme, ale, stock and treacle. Bring just to the boil, reduce the heat and cover with a lid. Bake in a preheated oven, 160°C (325°F), Gas Mark 3, for 1¼ hours or until the beef is tender. Check the seasoning and serve.

If liked, serve the casserole with mashed potatoes.

STICKY TOFFEE PUDDINGS

Serves 2
Preparation time 10 minutes
Cooking time 25—30 minutes

1 tablespoon **golden syrup**

1 tablespoon **black treacle**

1 tablespoon **double cream**

25 g (1 oz) **walnuts**, lightly toasted and ground

Essentials
vegetable oil, for brushing
75 g (3 oz) butter, softened
50 g (2 oz) caster sugar
1 egg, lightly beaten
50 g (2 oz) self-raising
  flour

Brush 2 ramekins, each holding 200 ml (7 fl oz), lightly with oil. In a small saucepan heat together the syrup, treacle and half of the butter until melted. Divide half the mixture between the prepared ramekins, stir double cream into the remainder and set aside.

Put the remaining butter and sugar in a food processor or blender and process briefly. Add the egg and flour and process again for 30 seconds. Stir in the walnuts.

Spoon the butter and sugar mixture into the ramekins to cover the syrup mixture. Stand the ramekins in a shallow roasting tin and bake in a preheated oven, 180°C (350°F), Gas Mark 4, for 25—30 minutes until risen and golden. Remove the ramekins from the oven and leave to stand for 5 minutes.

Meanwhile, heat the remaining treacle mixture. Unmould the puddings and pour over the treacle. Serve with custard or cream, if liked.

BREAD & BUTTER PUDDING

Serves 2
Preparation time 15 minutes, plus standing
Cooking time 30 minutes

2 thin slices of day-old **white bread**

25 g (1 oz) **sultanas**

grated rind of 1 **lemon**

Essentials
25 g (1 oz) butter, plus
  extra for greasing
300 ml (½ pint) milk
1 egg
1 egg yolk
15 g (½ oz) caster sugar
½ teaspoon grated nutmeg

Spread the bread slices with the butter and cut each into 4 triangles. Place a layer of bread in the base of a small, greased pie dish. Sprinkle the sultanas and lemon rind over the top and cover with the remaining bread triangles.

Beat together the milk, egg, egg yolk and sugar in a bowl and pour the mixture over the bread. Cover and leave to stand for 30 minutes.

Sprinkle nutmeg over the surface and bake in a preheated oven, 180°C (350°F), Gas Mark 4, for 30 minutes. Remove from the oven and serve hot.

If liked, heat 1 tablespoon jelly marmalade and brush it over the top of the pudding before serving with cream.

CHOCOLATE FONDUE

Serves 2
Preparation time 15 minutes
Cooking time 10 minutes

50 g (2 oz) **milk chocolate**

50 g (2 oz) **white chocolate**

75 ml (3 fl oz) **double cream**

200 g (7 oz) **strawberries**

Essentials
25 ml (1 fl oz) olive oil
   (preferably mild)

Melt the milk chocolate and white chocolate in
2 separate bowls over pans of simmering water,
each with half the cream and half the oil.

Pour each chocolate into a separate small, heatproof
bowl or mini fondue pot with a lighted tealight
candle underneath.

Serve the chocolate fondues with strawberries for
dipping. You could also use marshmallows and
amaretti biscuits if liked.

CHOCOLATE OVERLOAD

Serves 2

Preparation time 8 minutes

4 chocolate cream sandwich biscuits, crushed

250 ml (8 fl oz) chocolate cookie ice cream, softened

1 tablespoon **runny caramel** or **dulce de leche** (optional)

white or milk **chocolate shavings**, to decorate

Essentials

15 g (½ oz) butter, melted

Mix the crushed biscuits with the melted butter and press firmly into the base of 2 dessert dishes.

Scoop ice cream over the top of the biscuit base. Drizzle with the caramel or spoon over the dulce de leche (if used) and decorate with white or milk chocolate shavings. Serve immediately.

VICTORIA SPONGE

Makes 1 cake
Preparation time 15 minutes, plus cooling
Cooking time 20—25 minutes

1 teaspoon **vanilla extract**

Essentials
175 g (6 oz) butter, at room
temperature, plus extra for greasing
175 g (6 oz) caster sugar
3 eggs
175 g (6 oz) self-raising flour

Grease 2 cake tins, each 20 cm (8 inches) across, and line the bases and sides with greaseproof paper. Use a wooden spoon to beat together the butter and sugar until pale and creamy. Gradually beat in the eggs and vanilla extract, a little at a time, adding a tablespoon of flour with each addition to help prevent the mixture from curdling. Sift the remaining flour into the bowl and fold gently into the creamed mixture with a metal spoon, taking care not to knock out the air.

Carefully spoon the mixture into the prepared tins and bake in a preheated oven at 180°C (350°), Gas Mark 4, for 20—25 minutes until the cakes are well risen and feel springy when gently pressed. Turn the cakes on to a wire rack to cool.

When the cakes are cold sandwich them together with buttercream or with fresh cream and jam.

FROTHY HOT CHOCOLATE

Serves 1
Preparation time 2 minutes
Cooking time 3 minutes

1 teaspoon **cornflour**

4 squares **plain dark chocolate**

2 tablespoons **alcohol** of your choice, such as brandy, rum or vodka

1 teaspoon grated **chocolate**, to serve

Essentials
300 ml (½ pint) milk
1 teaspoon caster sugar

Put the cornflour in a jug and mix in 1 tablespoon milk to make a smooth paste. Add 200 ml (7 fl oz) of the milk, the sugar, the chocolate and the alcohol. Heat in a pan on the hob or microwave the mixture on high (900 watts) for 2 minutes. Pour the hot chocolate into a tall glass mug.

Heat the remaining milk and froth vigorously. Pour over the hot chocolate. Sprinkle over some grated chocolate and serve immediately.

PASTA & PIZZA

QUICK TOMATO PASTA SAUCE

Serves 2
Preparation time 2 minutes
Cooking time 10—12 minutes

200 g (7 oz) **dried pasta** of your choice

250 ml (8 fl oz) **passata** (sieved tomatoes)

Essentials
1 tablespoon olive oil
1 garlic clove, finely chopped
salt and pepper

Cook the pasta in a large saucepan of salted boiling water according to the instructions on the packet until it is al dente.

Meanwhile, heat the oil in a saucepan over a low heat. Add the garlic and cook, stirring, for 30 seconds. Increase the heat to high and quickly stir in the passata. Bring to the boil and season with salt and pepper, then reduce the heat and simmer for 5 minutes. Remove from the heat.

Drain the pasta thoroughly and stir into the sauce.

Serve immediately with a drizzle of olive oil or a scattering of grated Parmesan, if liked.

SPAGHETTI CARBONARA

Serves 2
Preparation time 10 minutes
Cooking time 15 minutes

75 g (3 oz) **smoked bacon**, rinded and cut into strips

150 g (5 oz) **spaghetti**

2 tablespoons **double cream**

50 g (2 oz) **Parmesan cheese**, grated

Essentials
1 tablespoon olive oil
1 garlic clove, crushed
2 egg yolks
salt and pepper

Heat the oil in a saucepan. Add the bacon and cook gently for 3 minutes. Add the garlic and cook for 1 minute.

Cook the spaghetti in a large saucepan of boiling water for 3—4 minutes if fresh or 8 minutes if dried, or according to the instructions on the packet until it is al dente. Drain and return the pasta to the pan.

Beat together the cream and egg yolks in a bowl, add to the bacon and mix well over a low heat. Add the sauce and Parmesan to the pasta, season with salt and pepper and toss well to combine. Serve immediately.

CLASSIC BASIL PESTO

Serves 2
Preparation time 2 minutes
Cooking time 10–12 minutes

200 g (7 oz) dried **spaghetti**

50 g (2 oz) **fresh basil leaves**

25 g (1 oz) **pine nuts**

25 g (1 oz) **Parmesan cheese**, freshly
grated, plus extra to serve

Essentials
1 garlic clove
50 ml (2 fl oz) olive oil
salt and pepper

Cook the pasta in a large saucepan of boiling water according to the instructions on the packet until it is al dente.

Meanwhile, put the basil, pine nuts and garlic in a food processor or blender and process until well blended. Transfer to a bowl and stir in the Parmesan and oil. Season to taste with salt and pepper.

Drain the pasta, reserving a ladleful of the cooking water, and return to the pan. Stir in the pesto, adding enough of the reserved pasta cooking water to loosen the mixture.

Serve immediately with a scattering of grated Parmesan.

BOLOGNESE SAUCE

Serves 4–6
Preparation time 15 minutes
Cooking time 1¼ hours

1 small **onion**, finely chopped
250 g (8 oz) lean **minced beef**
100 g (3¹/₂ oz) spicy **Italian sausages,**
skinned
200 g (7 oz) can **chopped tomatoes**

Essentials
15 g (½ oz) butter
1 tablespoon olive oil
1 garlic clove, crushed
150 ml (¼ pint) beef stock
1 teaspoon sugar
1 teaspoon dried oregano
1 tablespoon tomato purée
salt and pepper

Heat the butter and oil in a heavy-based saucepan. Add the onion and fry gently for 5 minutes. Add the garlic, beef and skinned sausages and cook until they are lightly coloured, breaking up the beef and the sausages with a wooden spoon.

Add the stock, tomatoes, sugar, oregano, tomato purée and a little salt and pepper and bring just to the boil. Reduce the heat to its lowest setting, cover the pan with a lid and cook for about 1 hour, stirring occasionally, to tenderize the meat and let the flavours mingle, until thick and pulpy.

If liked, serve with freshly cooked pasta.

EASY-COOK TOMATO SPAGHETTI

Serves 2
Preparation time 10 minutes, plus standing
Cooking time 10—12 minutes

375 g (12 oz) ripe **tomatoes**, quartered

5 **fresh basil leaves**

200 g (7 oz) dried **spaghetti**

150 g (5 oz) **mozzarella cheese**, cubed

Essentials
1 garlic clove, peeled
3 tablespoons olive oil
salt and pepper

Put the tomatoes, garlic and basil in a food processor or blender and process until the tomatoes are finely chopped but not smooth. Transfer to a bowl and add the oil. Season with salt and pepper. Leave the flavours to infuse for at least 15 minutes before cooking the pasta.

Cook the pasta in a large saucepan of salted boiling water according to the instructions on the packet until it is al dente.

Drain the pasta and stir into the prepared tomato sauce. Toss in the mozzarella and serve immediately.

CREAMY BLUE CHEESE PASTA

Serves 2
Preparation time 10 minutes
Cooking time 10 minutes

175 g (6 oz) dried **pasta shells**

3 **spring onions**, thinly sliced

75 g (3 oz) **dolcelatte cheese**, diced

100 g (3 1/2 oz) **cream cheese**

Essentials
1 tablespoon olive oil
salt and pepper

Cook the pasta shells in a large saucepan of salted boiling water according to the instructions on the packet until it is al dente.

Meanwhile, heat the oil in a frying pan, add the spring onions and cook over a medium heat for 2–3 minutes. Add the cheeses and stir until they blend into a smooth sauce.

Drain the pasta and transfer to a warm serving bowl. Stir in the sauce, season to taste with salt and pepper and serve immediately.

Serve garnished with snipped chives, if liked.

RED PEPPER & CHEESE TORTELLINI

Serves 2
Preparation time 10 minutes, plus cooling
Cooking time 15 minutes

1 red pepper

4 **spring onions**, finely sliced

250 g (8 oz) fresh **cheese-stuffed tortellini** or any other fresh stuffed tortellini of your choice

25 g (1 oz) **Parmesan cheese**, finely grated

Essentials
1 garlic clove, chopped
75 ml (3 fl oz) olive oil
salt and pepper

Cut the red pepper in quarters and remove the core and seeds. Lay the pieces, skin side up, under a preheated hot grill and cook until the skin blackens and blisters. Transfer to a plastic bag, tie the top and leave to cool. Peel away the skin.

Put the pepper flesh and garlic in a food processor or blender and process until fairly smooth. Stir in the spring onions and set aside.

Cook the pasta in a large saucepan of boiling water according to the instructions on the packet until it is al dente. Drain and return to the pan. Toss the pepper mixture into the pasta and add the oil and Parmesan. Season to taste with salt and pepper and serve immediately.

SAUSAGE MEATBALLS, PEAS & PASTA

Serves 2
Preparation time 20 minutes
Cooking time 15 minutes

250 g (8 oz) **beef or pork sausages,** skins removed

200 g (7 oz) dried **fusilli**

125 g (4 oz) frozen **peas,** thawed

Essentials
2 tablespoons olive oil
1 garlic clove, sliced
1—2 teaspoons dried sage
¼—½ teaspoon dried chilli
   flakes (to taste)
salt and pepper

Cut the sausagemeat into small pieces and roll into walnut-sized meatballs.

Heat half the oil in a nonstick frying pan, add the meatballs and cook over a medium heat, stirring requently, for 10 minutes until cooked through. Remove from the pan with a slotted spoon.

Meanwhile, cook the pasta in a large saucepan of lightly salted boiling water for 8 minutes. Add the peas, return to the boil and cook for a further 2 minutes until the peas are just tender and the pasta is al dente. Drain well, reserving 2 tablespoons of the cooking water.

Add the garlic, sage and chilli flakes to the meatball pan and season to taste with salt and pepper. Cook over a low heat for 2—3 minutes until the garlic is soft but not browned. Return the meatballs to the pan. Return the pasta and peas to the pan and stir in the meatball mixture, reserved cooking water and remaining oil and heat through for 2 minutes.

Serve in warm bowls topped with grated Parmesan, if liked.

TUNA NIÇOISE SPAGHETTI

Serves 2
Preparation time 10 minutes
Cooking time about 10 minutes

175 g (6 oz) dried **spaghetti**

200 g (7 oz) can **tuna** in oil, drained

50 g (2 oz) **green beans**, trimmed
and blanched

25 g (1 oz) pitted **kalamata olives**

Essentials
2 hard-boiled eggs
1 tablespoon lemon juice
salt and pepper

Shell and roughly chop the eggs and set them aside.
Cook the pasta in a large saucepan of lightly salted
boiling water according to the instructions on the
packet until it is al dente.

Mix together the tuna, beans, olives and lemon juice
in a bowl. Season to taste with pepper.

Drain the pasta and return to the pan. Add the tuna
mixture and gently toss to combine. Serve
immediately garnished with the chopped eggs.

CHORIZO CARBONARA

Serves 2
Preparation time 5 minutes
Cooking time 18–20 minutes

50 g (2 oz) **chorizo sausage**, sliced

175 g (6 oz) dried **penne**

25 g (1 oz) **Parmesan cheese**, grated, plus extra to serve

Essentials
1 tablespoon olive oil
2 eggs
salt and pepper

Heat the oil in a frying pan over a low heat. Add the chorizo and cook, turning occasionally, until crisp. (The melted fat released by the chorizo will be an essential part of the sauce.)

Cook the pasta in a large saucepan of lightly salted boiling water according to the instructions on the packet until it is al dente.

Meanwhile, put the eggs in a bowl with the Parmesan. Season to taste with salt and pepper and mix together with a fork.

Just before the pasta is ready, increase the heat under the frying pan so that the oil and melted chorizo fat start to sizzle. Drain the pasta thoroughly, return to the pan and immediately stir in the egg mixture and contents of the frying pan. Stir vigorously so that the eggs cook evenly. Serve immediately with a scattering of grated Parmesan.

BROCCOLI & SAUSAGE PASTA

Serves 2
Preparation time 5 minutes
Cooking time 15 minutes

1 small **onion**, finely chopped

100 g (3½ oz) Italian **pork sausage**

150 g (5 oz) dried **pasta**

100 g (3½ oz) **broccoli**, broken into florets

Essentials
1 tablespoon olive oil
pinch of crushed dried
 chillies
salt

Heat the oil in a frying pan. Add the onion and cook,
stirring occasionally, over a low heat for 6—7 minutes
until softened.

Split open the sausage and break up the sausagemeat
with a fork. Add the sausagemeat chunks and chillies
to the pan and increase the heat to medium. Cook,
stirring, for 4—5 minutes until the sausagemeat is
golden-brown.

Meanwhile, cook the pasta and broccoli in a large
saucepan of lightly salted boiling water according to
the instructions on the packet until it is al dente.
(Don't worry if the broccoli starts to break up; it
should be very tender.)

Drain the pasta and broccoli and toss into the frying
pan with the sausagemeat.

If liked, stir 25 g (1 oz) of grated pecorino cheese
into the sausagemeat mixture and serve with a bowl of
extra grated pecorino on the side.

PANCETTA & TOMATO BUCATINI

Serves 2
Preparation time 5 minutes
Cooking time 1 hour

1 small **onion**, finely chopped

50 g (2 oz) **pancetta**, cut into cubes

400 g (13 oz) can **chopped tomatoes**

200 g (7 oz) dried **bucatini**

Essentials
1 tablespoon olive oil
1 garlic clove, crushed
1—2 teaspoons dried red chilli
   flakes (to taste)
salt and pepper

Heat the oil in a frying pan. Add the onion and pancetta and cook over a low heat, stirring occasionally, for 7—8 minutes until the onion is soft and the pancetta is golden. Add the garlic and chilli and cook, stirring, for 1 minute, then stir in the tomatoes. Season to taste with salt and pepper and bring to the boil. Reduce the heat and simmer very gently for 40 minutes, adding a little water if the sauce begins to stick. (The sauce can be prepared ahead up to this stage, if you like.) Cook the pasta in a large saucepan of lightly salted boiling water according to the instructions on the packet until it is al dente. Drain, reserving a ladleful of the cooking water. Return the pasta to the saucepan.

If you have already prepared the sauce, heat it through gently before adding it to the pasta. Stir over a medium heat to combine, then add the reserved pasta cooking water and continue stirring until the pasta is well coated and looks silky.

Serve immediately with a scattering of grated Parmesan or pecorino cheese, if liked.

PENNE WITH SAUSAGE & TOMATO

Serves 2
Preparation time 5 minutes
Cooking time 45 minutes

1 small **onion**, finely chopped

125 g (4 oz) Italian **pork sausage**

300 g (10 oz) can **chopped tomatoes**

200 g (6 oz) dried **penne** or **rigatoni**

Essentials
1 tablespoon olive oil
½ teaspoon chilli powder
2 tablespoons milk
salt

Heat the oil in a frying pan. Add the onion and cook over a low heat, stirring occasionally, for 6–7 minutes until softened.

Split open the sausage and break up the sausagemeat with a fork. Add the sausagemeat chunks and chilli powder to the pan and increase the heat to medium. Cook, stirring, for 4–5 minutes, until the sausagemeat is golden-brown.

Stir in the tomatoes, season with salt and bring to the boil. Reduce the heat and simmer for about 25 minutes or until thick. Stir in the milk and simmer for a further 5 minutes.

Meanwhile, cook the pasta in a large saucepan of lightly salted boiling water according to the instructions on the packet until it is al dente. Drain the pasta and stir into the sauce.

Serve immediately with some grated Parmesan or pecorino cheese in a bowl, if liked.

SPICY TUNA, TOMATO & OLIVE PASTA

Serves 2
Preparation time 10 minutes
Cooking time 10—12 minutes

200 g (7 oz) dried **penne** or **rigatoni**

200 g (7 oz) ripe **tomatoes**, roughly chopped

25 g (1 oz) pitted **black olives**, roughly chopped

150 g (5 oz) can **tuna** in olive oil, drained

Essentials

1 tablespoon olive oil, plus extra to serve (optional)
1 garlic clove, thinly sliced
pinch of crushed dried chillies
2 teaspoons dried thyme
salt and pepper

Cook the pasta in a large saucepan of lightly salted boiling water according to instructions on the packet until it is al dente.

Meanwhile, heat the oil in a large frying pan. Add the garlic, chillies, tomatoes, olives and thyme and cook over a medium heat for a few minutes, then bring to the boil and simmer for 5 minutes.

Break up the tuna with a fork and stir into the sauce. Simmer for 2 minutes, then season to taste with salt and pepper.

Drain the pasta and toss into the sauce. Serve immediately, drizzled with a little olive oil, if liked.

WILD MUSHROOM PAPPARDELLE

Serves 2
Preparation time 15 minutes
Cooking time 12—25 minutes

175 g (6 oz) mixed **wild mushrooms**, cleaned

2 tablespoons roughly chopped **fresh flat leaf parsley**

200 g (7 oz) dried **pappardelle**

Essentials
3 tablespoons olive oil
1 garlic clove, thinly sliced
1 tablespoon lemon juice
25 g (1 oz) butter, diced
salt and pepper

Trim the mushrooms, slicing porcini mushrooms (if you can find some fresh) and tearing large, delicate mushrooms, such as chanterelles or oyster mushrooms. Heat the oil in a large, heavy-based frying pan over a low heat. Add the garlic and leave the flavours to infuse for 5 minutes. If the garlic begins to colour, simply remove the pan from the heat and leave to infuse in the warmth of the pan.

Increase the heat to high, add the mushrooms and cook, stirring, for 3—4 minutes until the mushrooms are tender and golden. Remove from the heat and stir in the lemon juice, parsley and butter. Season with salt and pepper.

Meanwhile, cook the pasta in a large saucepan of lightly salted boiling water according to the instructions on the packet until it is al dente. Drain thoroughly, reserving a ladleful of the cooking water. Return the pan with the mushroom mixture to a medium heat and stir in the pasta. Toss until well combined, then pour in the reserved pasta cooking water and continue stirring until the pasta is well coated.

Serve immediately with shavings of Parmesan cheese, if liked.

PASTA WITH GARLIC, OIL & CHILLI

Serves 2
Preparation time 5 minutes
Cooking time 8 minutes

200 g (7 oz) dried **spaghetti**

1 small **red chilli,** deseeded and chopped

2 tablespoons chopped **fresh parsley**

Essentials
50 ml (2 fl oz)
   olive oil
1 garlic clove,
   finely chopped
salt and pepper

Cook the pasta in a large saucepan of lightly salted boiling water according to the instructions on the packet until it is al dente.

Meanwhile, heat the oil in a saucepan over a low heat, add the garlic and a pinch of salt and cook, stirring constantly, until the garlic is golden. (If the garlic becomes too brown, it will taste bitter.) Stir in the chilli.

Drain the pasta and add to the saucepan with the warm but not sizzling garlic, oil and chilli. Add plenty of pepper and the parsley and toss to combine. Serve immediately.

FETTUCCINE AL' ALFREDO

Serves 2
Preparation time 5 minutes
Cooking time 5—15 minutes

200 g (7 oz) dried **fettuccine** or **tagliatelle**

100 ml (3¹/2 fl oz) **double cream**

25 g (1 oz) **Parmesan cheese**, freshly grated,
plus extra to serve

Essentials
25 g (1 oz) butter
large pinch of grated nutmeg
3 tablespoons milk
salt and pepper

Cook the pasta in a large saucepan of lightly salted
boiling water according to the instructions on the
packet until it is al dente.

Meanwhile, melt the butter in a heavy-based pan. Add
the cream and bring to the boil. Reduce the heat and
simmer for 1 minute until slightly thickened.

Drain the pasta thoroughly, then toss it into the
pan with the cream over a low heat. Add the nutmeg,
Parmesan and milk, and season with salt and pepper.
Toss gently until the sauce has thickened and the
pasta is well coated. Serve immediately with a
scattering of grated Parmesan.

MUSHROOM & SPINACH LASAGNE

Serves 2
Preparation time 15 minutes
Cooking time 12 minutes

250 g (8 oz) **mixed mushrooms,** sliced

100 g (3½ oz) **mascarpone cheese**

6 bought fresh **lasagne sheets**

50 g (2 oz) **baby spinach**

Essentials
1 tablespoon olive oil,
plus extra for oiling
salt and pepper

Heat the oil in a large frying pan. Add the mushrooms and cook over a medium heat, stirring frequently, for 5 minutes.

Add half the mascarpone and cook over a high heat for 1 minute until thickened. Season to taste with salt and pepper.

Meanwhile, put the pasta sheets in a large roasting tray and cover with boiling water. Leave to stand for 5 minutes or until tender. Drain off the water.

Lightly oil an ovenproof dish and place 1½ pasta sheets over the base, slightly overlapping. Top the pasta with a little of the remaining mascarpone, one-third of the mushroom sauce and one-third of the spinach. Repeat the process with 2 more layers, then top the final layer of pasta with the remaining mascarpone.

Put the lasagne under a preheated hot grill and cook for 5 minutes until the cheese is golden-brown. Serve immediately.

MACARONI CHEESE WITH BACON

Serves 2
Preparation time 5 minutes
Cooking time 30 minutes

125 g (4 oz) dried **macaroni**

50 g (2 oz) **smoked bacon**, diced

150 ml (1/4 pint) **double cream**

50 g (2 oz) **Cheddar cheese,** grated

Essentials
1 garlic clove, crushed
50 ml (2 fl oz) chicken stock
salt and pepper

Cook the pasta in a large saucepan of lightly salted boiling water according to the instructions on the packet until it is al dente.

Meanwhile, heat a dry frying pan until hot, add the bacon and cook for 3 minutes until browned and the fat is released. Remove from the pan with a slotted spoon. Add the garlic to the pan and cook gently for 2–3 minutes until soft.

Stir in the macaroni with the bacon, cream, stock and a little salt and pepper. Heat gently, stirring, for 2–3 minutes until warmed through. Stir in the cheese, remove the pan from the heat and stir until the cheese has melted.

Spoon the mixture into 2 ovenproof dishes, each holding 300 ml (½ pint), and bake in a preheated oven, 190°C (375°F), Gas Mark 5, for 12–15 minutes until bubbling and golden.

If liked, scatter 1 tablespoon grated Parmesan cheese over the top of each dish before baking. Serve with a green salad, if liked.

CHEESY PASTA & MUSHROOM BAKE

Serves 2
Preparation time 10 minutes
Cooking time 35—40 minutes

1 small **onion**, finely chopped

125 g (4 oz) **button mushrooms**, quartered

250 g (8 oz) ready-made **cheese sauce**

175 g (6 oz) dried **penne**

Essentials
2 tablespoons olive oil,
  plus extra for brushing
1 garlic clove, crushed
½ teaspoon dried sage
salt and pepper

Lightly brush 2 ovenproof dishes, each holding 300 ml (½ pint), with oil.

Heat half the olive oil in a frying pan. Add the onion, garlic and sage and cook gently for 10 minutes until softened. Season to taste with salt and pepper. Add the remaining oil, then increase the heat to high, add the mushrooms and cook, stirring, for 3—4 minutes until golden.

Add the cheese sauce and heat gently for 2—3 minutes until just bubbling.

Meanwhile, cook the pasta in a large saucepan of lightly salted boiling water according to the instructions on the packet until it is al dente. Drain well and return to the pan.

Stir the sauce into the pasta and season to taste with salt and pepper.

Spoon the pasta into the prepared dishes and bake in a preheated oven, 190°C (375°F), Gas Mark 5, for 15—20 minutes until bubbling and golden. Serve immediately.

CLASSIC TOMATO PIZZA

Makes 2 pizzas
Preparation time 10 minutes
Cooking time 30 minutes

1 onion, sliced finely
400 g (13 oz) can chopped tomatoes
2 ready-made pizza bases
125 g (4 oz) mozzarella cheese, sliced

Essentials
1 tablespoon olive oil
1 garlic clove, crushed
sugar (to taste)
salt and pepper

Heat the oil in a large saucepan. Add the onion and
garlic and cook for 3 minutes. Add the tomatoes,
vinegar and sugar. Season to taste with salt and
pepper. Increase the heat and simmer until the
mixture has reduced by half.

Put the pizza bases on warmed baking sheets, spoon
over the sauce and spread to the edge of the bases
with the back of the spoon. Arrange the mozzarella
on top.

Put the pizzas into a preheated oven, 230°C (450°F),
Gas Mark 8, for 10 minutes until golden and
sizzling. Serve immediately.

TUNA & PINEAPPLE PIZZA

Makes 2 pizzas
Preparation time 10 minutes
Cooking time 10 minutes

2 ready-made **pizza bases**

100 g (3 1/2 oz) can **pineapple**, drained and chopped

75 g (2 oz) can **tuna** in olive oil, drained and flaked

125 g (4 oz) **mozzarella cheese**, sliced

Essentials
1 garlic clove, halved
salt and pepper

Rub the top surfaces of the pizza bases with the cut faces of the garlic clove.

Put the pizza bases on warmed baking sheets, top with the pineapple and tuna, scatter over the mozzarella and bake in a preheated oven, 200°C (400°F), Gas Mark 6, for 10 minutes or until golden and bubbling. Season to taste with salt and pepper and serve immediately.

THREE-CHEESE PIZZA

Makes 2 pizzas
Preparation time 5 minutes
Cooking time 10 minutes

2 ready-made **pizza bases**
50 g (2 oz) **mozzarella cheese**, sliced
25 g (1 oz) **taleggio** or **fontina cheese**, diced
25 g (1 oz) **Gorgonzola cheese**, crumbled

Put the pizza bases on warm baking sheets.

Scatter half the cheeses over each pizza base.
Bake in a preheated oven, 200°C (400°F), Gas Mark 6,
for 10 minutes or until crisp and golden. Serve
immediately.

If liked, serve topped with rocket leaves.

TORTILLA PIZZA WITH SALAMI

Makes 2 pizzas
Preparation time 5 minutes
Cooking time 8–10 minutes

2 large **flour tortillas** or **flatbreads**

4 tablespoons ready-made **tomato pasta sauce**

100 g (3½ oz) **spicy salami**, sliced

150 g (5 oz) **mozzarella cheese**, thinly sliced

Essentials
salt and pepper

Put the tortillas or flatbreads on warm baking sheets. Top each with half the pasta sauce, spreading it to the edge. Arrange half the salami and mozzarella slices over the top of each.

Bake in a preheated oven, 200°C (400°F), Gas Mark 6, for 8–10 minutes or until the cheese is melted and golden. Season with salt and pepper and serve.

PIZZA BIANCHI

Makes 2 pizzas
Preparation time 5 minutes
Cooking time 6–7 minutes

2 x 20 cm (8 inch) **flatbreads**

200 g (7 oz) **Gorgonzola** or **dolcelatte cheese**, crumbled

8 slices of **prosciutto**

50 g (2 oz) **rocket**

Essentials
pepper
olive oil, for drizzling

Put the flatbreads on warm baking sheets and scatter the centres with the blue cheese. Bake in a preheated oven, 200°C (400°F), Gas Mark 6, for 6–7 minutes until the cheese has melted and the bases are crisp.

Top the pizzas with the prosciutto and some rocket. Grind over some fresh black pepper and drizzle with olive oil. Serve immediately.

FRENCH BREAD PIZZAS WITH SALAMI

Makes 2 pizzas
Preparation time 5 minutes
Cooking time 5—6 minutes

2 slices of **baguette**

3 tablespoons ready-made **tomato and basil pasta sauce**

50 g (2 oz) **mozzarella cheese**, sliced

50 g (2 oz) **pepperoni** or **salami**, sliced

Essentials
½ teaspoon dried oregano

Put the bread on a warm baking sheet and spread the tomato and basil sauce over it.

Top with the mozzarella, pepperoni or salami and scatter with oregano. Cook in a preheated oven, 200°C (400°F), Gas Mark 6, for 5—6 minutes until the cheese has melted. Serve immediately.

SPINACH & RICOTTA PITTA BREAD PIZZA

Makes 2 pizzas
Preparation time 5 minutes
Cooking time 8 minutes

2 wholemeal **pitta breads**

2–3 tablespoons ready-made **tomato pasta sauce**

50 g (2 oz) frozen **spinach**, thawed and squeezed dry

50 g (2 oz) **ricotta cheese**, crumbled

Essentials
2 tablespoons olive oil
salt and pepper

Put the pitta breads on a warm baking sheet and spread them with the tomato sauce. Top with small piles of spinach and scatter over the ricotta. Drizzle with olive oil and season with salt and pepper.

Cook in a preheated oven, 180°C (350°F), Gas Mark 4, for 8 minutes until crisp. Serve immediately.

SPICY CHICKEN NAAN BREAD PIZZAS

Makes 2 pizzas
Preparation time 5 minutes
Cooking time 10 minutes

2 ready-made plain or garlic **naan breads**

125 g (4 oz) ready-made **tandoori chicken**, sliced

100 g (3 1/2 oz) **cherry tomatoes**, halved

1/4 red **onion**, finely sliced

Essentials

- 2 tablespoons olive oil
- 1 garlic clove, crushed
- 1 tablespoon dried coriander

Put the olive oil, garlic and coriander in a small bowl and mix together. Put the naan breads on a warm baking sheet and scatter over the chicken, tomatoes and onion.

Drizzle over half the oil and bake in a preheated oven, 200°C (400°F), Gas Mark 6, for 10 minutes, until the naans are just crunchy. Drizzle over the remaining oil and serve immediately.

VEGETARIAN DISHES

ONION & MUSHROOM QUESADILLAS

Serves 2
Preparation time 10 minutes
Cooking time about 30 minutes

1 **onion**, thinly sliced

100 g (3¹/2 oz) **button mushrooms**, sliced

4 **flour tortillas**

50 g (2 oz) **Cheddar cheese**, grated

Essentials
2 tablespoons olive oil
½ teaspoon sugar
1½ teaspoons dried parsley
salt and pepper

Heat half the oil in a large frying pan. Add the onion and cook until soft. Add the sugar and cook for 3 minutes or until caramelized. Remove the onion with a slotted spoon and set aside.

Heat the remaining oil in the pan, add the mushrooms and cook for 3 minutes or until golden-brown. Set aside.

Heat a nonstick frying pan and add 1 tortilla. Scatter over half the onions, mushrooms, cheese and parsley. Season to taste with salt and pepper and cover with another tortilla. Cook until browned on the underside. Turn over and cook until browned on the other side.

Remove from the pan and keep warm while you repeat with the remaining ingredients.

Cut into wedges and serve with a salad, if liked.

RISI E BISI

Serves 2
Preparation time 5 minutes
Cooking time about 25 minutes

1 small **onion**, finely chopped
125 g (4 oz) **risotto rice**
225 g (7¹/2 oz) frozen **peas**
25 g (1 oz) **Parmesan cheese**, grated

Essentials
15 g (½ oz) butter
1 tablespoon olive oil
1 garlic clove, crushed
450 ml (¾ pint) hot vegetable stock
2 teaspoons dried parsley
salt and pepper

Melt the butter with the oil in a saucepan. Add the onion and garlic and cook until the onion is soft and starting to brown. Add the rice and stir until coated with the butter mixture.

Add the hot stock, a ladleful at a time, and cook, stirring constantly, until each addition has been absorbed before adding the next. Continue until all the stock has been absorbed and the rice is creamy and cooked but still retains a little bite; this will take around 15 minutes.

Add the peas and heat through for 3—5 minutes. Remove from the heat and stir in the Parmesan and parsley. Season to taste with salt and pepper and serve immediately.

SPINACH & LEMON RISOTTO

Serves 2
Preparation time 5 minutes
Cooking time 20 minutes

1 small **onion**, finely chopped

150 g (5 oz) **risotto rice**

250 g (8 oz) **spinach**, chopped

50 g (2 oz) **Parmesan cheese**, grated

Essentials
500 ml (17 fl oz) vegetable
  stock
50 g (2 oz) butter
1 tablespoon olive oil
2 tablespoons lemon juice
salt and pepper

Put the stock in a saucepan and simmer gently. Melt half of the butter with the oil in a heavy-based saucepan. Add the onion and sauté gently for 3 minutes. Add the rice and stir well to coat each grain with the butter and oil.

Add enough stock to just cover the rice and stir well. Simmer gently, stirring frequently. When almost all the liquid is absorbed, add more stock. Continue adding the stock in stages and stirring until it is absorbed.

Before you add the last of the stock, stir in the spinach, lemon juice and salt and pepper to taste. Increase the heat, stir well and add the remaining stock and butter. Allow to cook for a few minutes, then add half of the Parmesan and mix in well. Serve scattered with the remaining Parmesan.

COURGETTE & HERB RISOTTO

Serves 2
Preparation time 10 minutes
Cooking time about 25 minutes

1 small **onion**, finely chopped

175 g (6 oz) **risotto rice**

50 g (2 oz) **courgettes**, finely diced

25 g (1 oz) **Parmesan cheese**, finely grated

Essentials
30 g (1¼ oz) butter
1 tablespoon olive oil
1 garlic clove, finely chopped
750 ml (1¼ pints) hot vegetable stock
1 teaspoon dried herbs
salt and pepper

Heat the butter and oil in a saucepan. Add the onion and garlic and cook for about 3 minutes until soft. Add the rice and stir until coated.

Add the hot stock, a ladleful at a time, and cook, stirring constantly, until each addition has been absorbed before adding the next. Continue until all the stock has been absorbed and the rice is creamy and cooked but still retains a little bite; this will take around 20 minutes.

Stir in the courgettes and heat through for 3—5 minutes. Remove from the heat and stir in the Parmesan and herbs. Season to taste with salt and pepper and serve immediately.

TOMATO & LEEK RICE

Serves 2
Preparation time 10 minutes, plus standing
Cooking time about 20 minutes

1 leek, sliced
200 g (7 oz) can chopped tomatoes
125 g (4 oz) long-grain rice

Essentials
1 tablespoon olive oil
1 garlic clove, crushed
325 ml (11 fl oz) vegetable stock
salt and pepper

Heat the oil in a saucepan. Add the leek and garlic and cook over a medium heat for a few minutes until soft and starting to brown. Add the tomatoes and rice and cook, stirring, for 1 minute.

Add the stock and season to taste with salt and pepper. Reduce the heat, cover tightly and cook for 12–15 minutes or until all the stock has been absorbed and the rice is tender.

Remove from the heat and leave to stand, covered, for 10 minutes. Stir, then serve immediately.

MIXED BEAN KEDGEREE

Serves 2
Preparation time 10 minutes
Cooking time 15—20 minutes

1 small **onion**, chopped

125 g (4 oz) **long-grain rice**

400 g (13 oz) can **mixed beans**, rinsed and drained

75 ml (3 fl oz) **soured cream**

Essentials
1 tablespoon olive oil
1 tablespoon medium curry paste
375 ml (13 fl oz) vegetable stock
2 eggs
salt and pepper

Heat the oil in a saucepan. Add the onion and cook until soft. Stir in the curry paste and rice. Add the stock and season to taste with salt and pepper. Bring to the boil, then reduce the heat, cover and simmer, stirring occasionally, for 10—15 minutes until all the stock has been absorbed and the rice is tender.

Meanwhile, put the eggs in a saucepan of cold water and bring to the boil. Cook for 10 minutes, then plunge into cold water to cool. Shell the eggs and cut them into wedges.

Stir the beans and soured cream through the rice mixture and cook briefly over a low heat to heat through. Serve garnished with the eggs.

POTATO GRATIN

Serves 2
Preparation time 10 minutes
Cooking time 40 minutes

750 g (1½ lb) floury **potatoes**, sliced

1 small **onion**, sliced

275 g (9 oz) **Cheddar cheese**, grated

200 ml (7 fl oz) **double cream** or full-fat crème fraîche

Essentials
25 g (1 oz) butter, plus extra for greasing
1 tablespoon olive oil
1 garlic clove, finely chopped
salt and pepper

Cook the potatoes in lightly salted boiling water for 10 minutes and drain.

Heat the butter and oil in a medium saucepan. Cook the onion for about 5 minutes or until soft and golden. Add the garlic and cook for a further 2 minutes.

Add half the cheese and the cream or crème fraîche. Stir until the mixture is hot and the cheese has melted. Season to taste with salt and pepper.

Arrange half the potatoes in a lightly buttered, shallow, ovenproof dish. Pour over half the cheese sauce. Cover with the remaining potato slices, the rest of the cheese sauce and top with the remaining cheese.

Cook in a preheated oven, 220°C (425°F), Gas Mark 7, for 30 minutes or until bubbling and golden-brown.

Serve immediately with a salad, if liked.

AUBERGINE & MOZZARELLA BAKE

Serves 2
Preparation time 15 minutes
Cooking time 25—30 minutes

1 large **aubergine**, about 500 g (1 lb)

1 small jar ready-made **tomato sauce**

125 g (4 oz) **mozzarella cheese**, grated

25 g (1 oz) **Parmesan cheese**, grated

Essentials
2 tablespoons olive oil, plus
  extra for oiling
salt and pepper

Cut the aubergine into thin slices, brush the slices
with the oil and season with a little salt and
pepper. Arrange them on a foil-lined grill pan and
cook under a preheated hot grill for 2—3 minutes on
each side until charred and softened.

Lightly brush an ovenproof dish with oil. Layer the
aubergine slices, tomato sauce and mozzarella in the
dish to give 3 layers of each, ending with the
mozzarella. Scatter over the Parmesan.

Bake in a preheated oven, 200°C (400°F), Gas Mark 6,
for 20—25 minutes until bubbling and golden.

If liked, serve with a crisp green salad and some
crusty bread.

POTATO & CAULIFLOWER CURRY

Serves 2
Preparation time 15 minutes
Cooking time 20–30 minutes

1 small **onion**, finely chopped

125 g (4 oz) **potatoes**, diced

125 g (4 oz) **cauliflower**, cut into chunks

2 **tomatoes**, skinned and chopped

Essentials
2 tablespoons vegetable oil
1 teaspoon cumin seeds
about 1 teaspoon chilli powder (to taste)
½ teaspoon ground turmeric
salt

Heat the oil in a heavy-based saucepan. Add the onion and cook over a medium heat, stirring occasionally, for about 10 minutes or until golden. Add the cumin seeds and cook, stirring frequently, until they sizzle.

Add the potatoes, cauliflower, chilli powder and turmeric. Season to taste with salt. Cook, stirring constantly, for 2–3 minutes.

Stir in the tomatoes. To make a dry vegetable curry add 1–2 tablespoons water, cover and cook gently for 10–12 minutes until dry. For a moister curry stir in 4–5 tablespoons water, cover and simmer for 5–6 minutes until the vegetables are tender.

If liked, serve as a main dish with naan bread, chapattis or basmati rice or on its own as a side dish.

CHICKPEA & TOMATO CASSEROLE

Serves 2
Preparation time 10 minutes
Cooking time about 30 minutes

500 g (1 lb) **tomatoes**, halved
1 small **onion**, chopped
1 **red chilli**, deseeded and chopped
410 g (13 1/2 oz) can **chickpeas**, rinsed and drained

Essentials
2 garlic cloves, crushed
2 teaspoons dried rosemary
olive oil, for greasing
25 ml (1 fl oz) vegetable stock
salt and pepper

Arrange the tomatoes in a roasting tin, scatter over the garlic and half the rosemary and stir to combine. Cook in a preheated oven, 200°C (400°F), Gas Mark 6, for 30 minutes.

Meanwhile, lightly brush an ovenproof casserole dish with oil and gently cook the onion for 10 minutes. Add the remaining rosemary, chilli, stock and chickpeas, season to taste with salt and pepper, cover and transfer to the oven for 20 minutes or the remainder of the tomato cooking time.

When the tomatoes are cooked, stir them into the chickpeas with all the juices from the roasting tin. Check the seasoning and serve.

If liked, serve with baked potatoes and a green salad.

GNOCCHI WITH SAGE BUTTER

Serves 2
Preparation time 30 minutes
Cooking time 15—18 minutes

250 g (8 oz) floury **potatoes**, cubed

1 tablespoon chopped **fresh sage**

Essentials
1 small egg, beaten
1 tablespoon olive oil
75 g (3 oz) plain flour
50 g (2 oz) butter
salt

Cook the potatoes in a saucepan of lightly salted boiling water for 10—12 minutes until tender. Drain, return the potatoes to the pan and heat gently for several seconds to dry out. Mash the potatoes and beat in the egg, ½ teaspoon salt, the oil and the flour to form a sticky dough.

Take walnut-sized pieces of the dough and roll into egg shapes, rolling them over the tines of a fork. Bring a large saucepan of lightly salted water to a rolling boil, add half the gnocchi (freeze the remainder for later use) and cook for 3 minutes until they rise to the surface. Drain and transfer to warm serving bowls.

Meanwhile, melt the butter in a frying pan. As soon as it stops foaming, add the sage and fry over a medium-high heat, stirring, for 2—3 minutes until crisp and the butter turns golden-brown. Drizzle over the gnocchi, scatter with grated Parmesan, if liked, and serve immediately.

ROASTED STUFFED PEPPERS

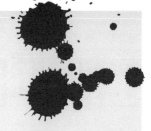

Serves 2
Preparation time 10 minutes
Cooking time about 1 hour

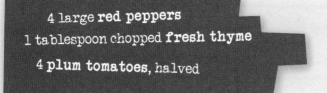

4 large **red peppers**

1 tablespoon chopped **fresh thyme**

4 **plum tomatoes**, halved

Essentials
2 garlic cloves, crushed
4 tablespoons olive oil
2 tablespoons balsamic vinegar
salt and pepper

Cut the red peppers in half lengthways, scoop out and discard the cores and seeds. Put the pepper halves, cut sides up, in a foil-lined roasting tin or a ceramic dish. Divide the garlic and thyme between them and season to taste with salt and pepper.

Put a tomato half in each pepper and drizzle with the oil and vinegar. Roast in a preheated oven, 220°C (425°F), Gas Mark 7, for 55 minutes—1 hour until the peppers are soft and charred.

Serve with some crusty bread to mop up the juices and a baby leaf salad, if liked.

BAKED VEGETABLE FRITTATA

Serves 2
Preparation time 15 minutes
Cooking time 25 minutes

125 g (4 oz) **asparagus**, trimmed and halved
1 **leek**, trimmed and sliced
1 tablespoon chopped **fresh basil**
1 tablespoon grated **Parmesan cheese**

Essentials
1 tablespoon olive oil, plus
  extra for greasing
1 garlic clove, crushed
3 eggs
1 tablespoon milk
salt and pepper

Cook the asparagus in a saucepan of lightly salted boiling water for 2 minutes. Drain and shake dry. Meanwhile, heat the oil in a frying pan. Add the leek and garlic and fry gently for 5 minutes until they have softened. Add the asparagus and basil and remove the pan from the heat.

Beat the eggs with the milk and season with salt and pepper. Stir in the vegetable mixture and pour into a greased 600 ml (1 pint) ovenproof dish. Scatter over the Parmesan and cook in a preheated oven, 200°C (400°F), Gas Mark 6, for 15—20 minutes until firm in the centre. Serve warm, cut into wedges.

TOMATO, TAPENADE & FETA TART

Makes 1 tart
Preparation time 15 minutes
Cooking time 15—18 minutes

1 sheet of ready-rolled frozen **puff pastry,**
about 25 cm (10 inches) square, thawed

2 tablespoons **olive tapenade**

250 g (8 oz) **cherry tomatoes,** halved

100 g (3½ oz) **feta cheese,** diced

Essentials
2 tablespoons olive
  oil
pepper

Trim the edges of the pastry square, then use the
blade of a sharp knife to gently tap the edges to help
the pastry rise. Prick all over the surface of the
pastry with a fork and place it on a baking sheet.

Spread the pastry with the tapenade, leaving a 1 cm
(½ inch) border. Scatter over the tomatoes and feta.
Season with pepper and place the baking sheet on a
second preheated baking sheet.

Cook in a preheated oven, 220°C (425°F), Gas Mark 7,
for 15—18 minutes until golden. Drizzle the oil over
the tart before serving.

Serve with a fresh green salad, if liked.

SPICY POLENTA WITH HERBS

Serves 2
Preparation time 15 minutes
Cooking time about 10 minutes

75 g (3 oz) **polenta**

1 tablespoon chopped mixed **fresh herbs**, such as basil, chives, parsley and thyme

25 g (1 oz) grated **Parmesan cheese**

Essentials
25 g (1 oz) butter
1 garlic clove, crushed
pinch of dried red chilli flakes
salt and pepper

Bring 450 ml (¾ pint) water and ½ teaspoon salt to a rolling boil in a large saucepan.

Meanwhile, melt half the butter and fry the garlic and chilli flakes for about 1 minute until soft but not golden. Remove from the heat.

Gradually whisk the polenta into the boiling water in a steady stream. Add the garlic and chilli flakes with any butter in the pan and the herbs. Cook, stirring, over a low heat for 8—10 minutes until the polenta has thickened and is beginning to leave the sides of the pan.

Remove from the heat and beat in the remaining butter and cheese. Season to taste with salt and pepper. Spoon into warm bowls and serve immediately.

If liked, serve with extra grated Parmesan cheese and a green salad.

CURRIED RED LENTILS

Serves 2
Preparation time 15 minutes
Cooking time about 25 minutes

1 small **onion**, chopped

1 teaspoon grated **fresh root ginger**

200 g (7 oz) can **chopped tomatoes**

125 g (4 oz) dried **red lentils**

Essentials
1 garlic clove, chopped
2 tablespoons vegetable oil
about ½ tablespoon medium curry powder (to taste)
½ teaspoon ground turmeric
½ teaspoon ground cinnamon
300 ml (½ pint) vegetable stock
salt and pepper

Put the onion, garlic and ginger in a food processor or blender and process until smooth.

Heat the oil in a saucepan. Add the onion purée and spices and fry gently for about 5 minutes.

Add the tomatoes, lentils and stock, bring to the boil, cover and simmer over a low heat for about 20 minutes, until the lentils are cooked and the sauce has thickened. Season to taste with salt and pepper and serve immediately.

Serve with spoonfuls of Greek yogurt, if liked.

BUTTER BEAN & TOMATO CASSEROLE

Serves 2
Preparation time 15 minutes
Cooking time 25 minutes

1 **onion**, sliced

2 x 410 g (13½ oz) cans **butter beans**, rinsed and drained

400 g (13 oz) can **chopped tomatoes**

Essentials
vegetable oil, for greasing
1 garlic clove, crushed
125 ml (4 fl oz) vegetable stock
pinch of paprika
1 bay leaf
salt and pepper

Brush a flameproof casserole pan with oil. Add the onion and cook over a low heat for 10 minutes. Add the garlic and butter beans and stir to combine. Add all the remaining ingredients, season to taste with salt and pepper and bring to a simmer. Simmer for 15 minutes. Check the seasoning, remove the bay leaf and sprinkle with chopped parsley, if liked. Serve immediately.

If liked, serve with a green salad.

SWEETCORN & PEPPER FRITTATA

Serves 2
Preparation time 10 minutes
Cooking time about 10 minutes

2 **spring onions**, thinly sliced

100 g (3½ oz) can **sweetcorn**, drained

75 g (3 oz) bottled **roasted red peppers** in oil, drained and cut into strips

50 g (2 oz) strong **Cheddar cheese**, grated

Essentials
1 tablespoon olive oil
2 eggs, lightly beaten
salt and pepper

Heat the oil in a frying pan. Add the spring onions, sweetcorn and red peppers and cook for 30 seconds. Add the eggs and cheese and season to taste with salt and pepper. Cook over a medium heat for 4–5 minutes until the base is set.

Remove from the hob, place under a preheated grill and cook for 3–4 minutes or until golden and set. Serve immediately cut into wedges.

If liked, serve with crusty bread or a green salad.

SPINACH, FETA & EGG TARTS

Makes 4 tarts
Preparation time 15 minutes
Cooking time 16–18 minutes

250 g (8 oz) frozen **leaf spinach**, thawed

125 g (4 oz) **feta cheese**, diced

2 tablespoons **mascarpone cheese**

4 sheets of **filo pastry** (thawed if frozen)

Essentials
50 g (2 oz) butter, melted
4 eggs
salt and pepper

Drain the spinach and squeeze out the water, then chop
finely. Put the spinach in a bowl and mix in the feta
and mascarpone. Season to taste with salt and pepper.

Lay the sheets of filo pastry on top of one another,
brushing each with a little melted butter. Using
a saucer as a guide, cut out 4 rounds, each 15 cm
(6 inches) across.

Spoon the spinach mixture on to the pastry rounds,
spreading the filling out but leaving a 2.5 cm (1 inch)
border. Gather the edges up and over the filling to form
a rim. Make a shallow depression in the spinach mixture.

Transfer the tarts to a baking sheet and bake in
a preheated oven, 200°C (400°F), Gas Mark 6, for
8 minutes.

Remove from the oven and carefully crack an egg into
each hollow. Return to the oven and bake for a further
8–10 minutes until the eggs are set.

PEA & LEEK OMELETTE

Serves 2
Preparation time 5–6 minutes
Cooking time 19–22 minutes

125 g (4 oz) baby **new potatoes**

250 g (8 oz) **leeks**, trimmed and cut into 1 cm (1/2 inch) slices

100 g (3½ oz) frozen **peas**

50 g (2 oz) soft **garlic and chive cheese**

Essentials
40 g (1½ oz) butter
1 tablespoon olive oil
3 eggs
75 ml (3 fl oz) milk
salt and pepper

Cook the potatoes in boiling water for about 10 minutes or until cooked but still firm.

Meanwhile, melt the butter with the oil in a large frying pan. Add the leeks, cover and cook, stirring frequently, for 8–10 minutes or until soft. Stir in the peas.

Drain the potatoes, cut them into quarters and add to the frying pan. Continue cooking for 2–3 minutes. Whisk the eggs with the milk, season well with salt and pepper and pour into the frying pan. Move around with a spatula so that the vegetables are well coated and the egg begins to cook. Crumble the cheese on top and leave over a medium heat for 2–3 minutes until the egg becomes firm.

Place under a preheated hot grill for 3–4 minutes until the omelette is completely set and the top is golden-brown. Serve in thick slices.

ASIAN DISHES

THAI GREEN PORK CURRY

Serves 2
Preparation time 10 minutes
Cooking time 20 minutes

2 boneless **pork steaks**, cut into bite-sized pieces

1 tablespoon Thai **green curry paste**

200 ml (7 fl oz) **coconut milk**

100 g (3 1/2 oz) can **water chestnuts**, rinsed, drained and halved

Essentials
1 tablespoon olive oil

Heat the oil in a saucepan. Add the pork and cook, stirring, for 3–4 minutes until browned all over. Add the curry paste and cook, stirring, for 1 minute until fragrant.

Add the coconut milk, stir and reduce the heat to a gentle simmer. Cook for 10 minutes, then add the water chestnuts. Cook for a further 3 minutes. Serve immediately.

If liked, serve with plain boiled rice.

FAST CHICKEN CURRY

Serves 2
Preparation time 5 minutes
Cooking time 20—25 minutes

1 small **onion**, finely chopped

4 boneless, skinless **chicken thighs**, cut into thin strips

200 g (7 oz) can **chopped tomatoes**

50 ml (2 fl oz) **coconut milk**

Essentials

2 tablespoons olive oil

2 tablespoons medium curry paste

salt and pepper

Heat the oil in a deep nonstick saucepan. Add the onion and cook for 3 minutes until soft. Add the curry paste and cook, stirring, for 1 minute.

Add the chicken, tomatoes and coconut milk to the pan. Bring to the boil, then reduce the heat, cover and cook over a low heat for 15—20 minutes.

Remove from the heat, season well with salt and pepper and serve immediately with boiled rice, if liked.

COCONUT CHICKEN

Serves 2
Preparation time 10 minutes
Cooking time 20 minutes

1 small **onion**, diced

4 boneless, skinless **chicken thighs**, cut into bite-sized pieces

1/2 teaspoon finely chopped **fresh root ginger**

200 ml (7 fl oz) **coconut milk**

Essentials
1 tablespoon vegetable oil
1 tablespoon medium curry paste
1 garlic clove, crushed
1—2 teaspoons soy sauce (to taste)
salt and pepper (optional)

Heat the oil in a saucepan. Add the onion and cook for 5 minutes until soft and just starting to brown. Add the chicken and cook for 5 minutes until browned all over.

Add the curry paste, ginger, garlic and soy sauce and cook, stirring, for 2—3 minutes. Add the coconut milk and stir well. Cover and simmer gently for 5—8 minutes.

Remove from the heat. Season to taste with salt and pepper, if necessary, and serve immediately.

If liked, serve with boiled basmati rice.

TANDOORI CHICKEN

Serves 2
Preparation time 5 minutes, plus marinating
Cooking time 25—30 minutes

8 **chicken pieces,** such as drumsticks or thighs

1 tablespoon **tikka spice mix** or paste

50 ml (2 fl oz) **natural yogurt**

Essentials
1 garlic clove, crushed
2 teaspoons tomato purée
2 tablespoons lemon juice

Make deep slashes all over the chicken pieces. In a large non-metallic bowl mix together all the remaining ingredients. Add the chicken and turn to coat thoroughly with the marinade. Cover and leave to marinate in the refrigerator for at least 30 minutes or overnight.

Transfer the chicken to an ovenproof dish and cook in a preheated oven, 240°C (475°F), Gas Mark 9, for 25—30 minutes until cooked through, tender and lightly charred at the edges.

If liked, serve with plain rice or couscous.

TERIYAKI CHICKEN

Serves 2
Preparation time 10 minutes, plus marinating
Cooking time 8 minutes

1 boneless, skinless **chicken breast**, cut into thin strips

1 large **carrot**, peeled and cut into small matchsticks

1 **red pepper**, cored, deseeded and cut into small matchsticks

100 g (3½ oz) ready-made **teriyaki stir-fry sauce**

Essentials

1 tablespoon soy sauce

1 tablespoon olive oil

Put the chicken in a non-metallic bowl. Add the soy sauce and toss well to coat. Cover and leave to marinate in a cool place for 10 minutes.

Heat the oil in a wok or large frying pan, add the chicken and the juices from the bowl and stir-fry for 2 minutes. Add the carrots and peppers and stir-fry for 4 minutes. Add the sauce and cook briefly, stirring, to heat through. Serve immediately.

If liked, serve over egg noodles.

RICE NOODLES WITH LEMON CHICKEN

Serves 2
Preparation time 10 minutes
Cooking time 10 minutes

2 boneless **chicken breasts**, skin on

125 g (4 oz) dried **rice noodles**

small bunch of **fresh coriander**, chopped

Essentials
4 tablespoons lemon
   juice
2 tablespoons sweet
   chilli sauce
salt and pepper

Mix the chicken with half the lemon juice and the sweet chilli sauce in a large bowl and season to taste with salt and pepper.

Lay a chicken breast between 2 sheets of clingfilm and lightly pound with a mallet to flatten. Repeat with the other piece of chicken. Arrange the chicken on a grill rack and cook under a preheated grill for 4—5 minutes on each side or until cooked through. Finish on the skin side so that it is crisp.

Meanwhile, put the noodles in a heatproof bowl, pour over boiling water to cover and leave for 10 minutes until just tender, then drain.

Add the remaining lemon juice and coriander to the noodles and toss well to mix. Season to taste with salt and pepper. Top the noodles with the cooked chicken and serve immediately.

BEEF WITH BLACK BEAN SAUCE

Serves 2
Preparation time 15 minutes
Cooking time 15 minutes

325 g (11 oz) **minute steak**

1 small **onion**, thinly sliced

50 g (2 oz) **mangetout**, halved lengthways

100 g (3 1/2 oz) ready-made **black bean sauce**

Essentials

1 tablespoon vegetable oil
1 garlic clove, finely chopped
1—2 teaspoons dried chilli flakes (to taste)
salt and pepper

Trim the steak to remove all fat and then cut the meat into thin slices across the grain.

Heat half the oil in a wok or large frying pan, add the beef and cook, stirring, until browned all over. Transfer to a bowl.

Heat the remaining oil in the pan, add the onion and mangetout and stir-fry for 2 minutes. Add the garlic and chilli flakes and stir-fry for 1 minute.

Add the black bean sauce and cook, stirring, for 5 minutes or until the sauce begins to thicken. Season to taste with salt and pepper and serve immediately.

If liked, serve with plain boiled rice or egg-fried rice.

SESAME PRAWNS WITH PAK CHOI

Serves 2
Preparation time 10 minutes, plus marinating
Cooking time about 3 minutes

300 g (10 oz) large frozen **peeled prawns,** thawed

1 teaspoon **sesame oil**

2 teaspoons clear **honey**

250 g (8 oz) **pak choi**

Essentials
1 tablespoon soy sauce
½ teaspoon crushed garlic
2 teaspoons lemon juice
1 tablespoon vegetable oil
salt and pepper

Put the prawns in a non-metallic bowl. Add the sesame oil, soy sauce, honey, garlic and lemon juice. Season to taste with salt and pepper and mix well. Cover and leave to marinate in a cool place for 5–10 minutes.

Cut the heads of pak choi in half lengthways, then blanch in a large saucepan of boiling water for 40–50 seconds. Drain well, cover and keep warm.

Heat the vegetable oil in a wok or large frying pan. Add the prawns and the marinade from the bowl and stir-fry over a high heat for 2 minutes until hot. Arrange the pak choi on warm serving plates, top with the prawns and any juices from the pan and serve immediately.

TEA-SMOKED SALMON

Serves 2
Preparation time 10 minutes, plus marinating
Cooking time 15 minutes

2 skinless **salmon fillets**, each about 125 g (4 oz)

75 g (3 oz) uncooked **rice**

25 g (1 oz) **green tealeaves**

Essentials
1 tablespoon olive oil
50 g (2 oz) sugar
3 teaspoons salt

Mix together the oil, sugar and salt. Lay the salmon on a plate and rub it all over with the olive oil mixture. Cover and chill in the refrigerator for 1 hour, then wipe all the marinade off the salmon and discard.

Prepare the wok for smoking by lining it with foil. Mix together the rice and tealeaves and put them in the wok. Place a circular rack in the wok and place the wok over a high heat with the lid on. Heat until smoke starts to emerge.

Remove the lid and place the salmon on the rack. Replace the lid and cook for 2 minutes. Reduce the heat to medium and cook for a further 4 minutes. Turn off the heat and leave the salmon to sit in the wok for a further 6 minutes.

Serve the salmon with lemon wedges, a small bowl of mayonnaise and some salad leaves, if liked.

THAI RED PORK & BEAN CURRY

Serves 2
Preparation time 10 minutes
Cooking time 5 minutes

1 tablespoon Thai **red curry paste**

175 g (6 oz) lean **pork**, sliced into thin strips

100 g (3½ oz) **French beans**, topped and cut in half

1 tablespoon Thai **fish sauce** (nam pla)

Essentials
1 tablespoon
   vegetable oil
½ teaspoon sugar

Heat the oil in a wok over a medium heat until the oil starts to shimmer. Add the curry paste and cook, stirring, until it releases its aroma.

Add the pork and French beans and stir-fry for 2—3 minutes until the meat is cooked through and the beans are just tender. Stir in the fish sauce and sugar and serve.

If liked, serve with plain boiled rice.

CRISPY SPICED CHICKEN WINGS

Serves 2
Preparation time 5 minutes
Cooking time 8 minutes

6 chicken wings

1 small **red chilli**, deseeded and thinly sliced

2 **spring onions**, thinly sliced

2 teaspoons finely chopped **fresh root ginger**

Essentials
50 g (2 oz) plain flour
1—2 teaspoons chilli powder (to taste)
½ teaspoon salt
vegetable oil, for deep-frying
sweet chilli sauce, for dipping

Put the flour, chilli powder and salt in a large bowl and mix together thoroughly. Add the chicken wings and toss well to coat in the flour.

Pour enough oil into a wok or deep saucepan to deep-fry the chicken, and heat it to 190°C (375°F) or until a cube of bread dropped into the oil turns golden in 20 seconds. Deep-fry the chicken wings for 6—7 minutes, turning them in the oil until golden and crisp, then remove using a slotted spoon and drain on kitchen paper. Use a slotted spoon to lower the chilli, spring onions and ginger into the oil and sizzle until crisp and the chilli is a vibrant red. Drain thoroughly on kitchen paper.

Pile the chicken wings on to a warm serving plate. Scatter with the crispy chilli, spring onions and ginger and serve with sweet chilli sauce.

VEGETABLES IN YELLOW BEAN SAUCE

Serves 2
Preparation time 5 minutes
Cooking time 6–7 minutes

1/2 teaspoon chopped **fresh root ginger**

100 g (3 1/2 oz) can **bamboo shoots,** drained and sliced

150 g (5 oz) **broccoli** florets

1 tablespoon **yellow bean sauce**

Essentials
1 tablespoon vegetable oil
1 garlic clove, thinly sliced
generous pinch of salt

Heat the oil in a wok or large saucepan over a high heat until the oil starts to shimmer. Stir in the ginger, garlic and salt and stir-fry for 30 seconds. Add the bamboo shoots and broccoli and stir-fry for 2 minutes.

Stir in the yellow bean sauce and cook for 1 minute, then add 6 tablespoons water. Continue stir-frying until the vegetables are coated in a rich velvety sauce. Serve immediately.

If liked, serve with plain boiled rice.

BAMBOO CHICKEN WITH CASHEWS

Serves 2
Preparation time 10 minutes
Cooking time 15 minutes

200 g (7 oz) boneless, skinless **chicken breasts**, cubed

1 tablespoon **yellow bean sauce**

1 teaspoon **cornflour**

50 g (2 oz) **cashew nuts**, toasted

Essentials
125 ml (4 fl oz) chicken stock

Heat the stock in a wok or large frying pan. Add the chicken and bring the stock to the boil, stirring, then lower the heat and cook for 5 minutes. Remove the chicken with a slotted spoon and set aside. Add the yellow bean sauce to the wok and cook for 6 minutes.

Mix the cornflour to a smooth paste with 1–2 tablespoons water. Return the chicken to the wok, bring the sauce back to the boil and thicken with the cornflour paste. Stir in the cashew nuts just before serving with rice or noodles, if liked.

CHINESE FRIED RICE

Serves 2
Preparation time 15 minutes
Cooking time 5 minutes

75 g (3 oz) can mixed **peas and carrots**, drained

125 g (4 oz) cooked peeled **prawns**

200 g (7 oz) cooked **basmati rice**

3 **spring onions**, trimmed and sliced

Essentials
1½ tablespoons vegetable oil
1 egg, beaten
1—2 teaspoons soy sauce
   (to taste)

Heat a wok or large saucepan over a high heat until smoking. Add 1 tablespoon oil, heat again and add the carrot and peas. Stir-fry for 2 minutes, then add the prawns and rice and stir-fry for 2 minutes.

Make a well in the centre and add the egg. Stir the egg for 1 minute or until lightly scrambled, then mix it with the rice and prawns. Add the soy sauce, spring onions and remaining oil and take off the heat. Mix all together thoroughly before serving.

STIR-FRIED HOISIN BEANS

Serves 2
Preparation time 5 minutes
Cooking time about 5 minutes

250 g (8 oz) **French beans**, trimmed

1 large **red chilli**, halved, deseeded and sliced

3 tablespoons **hoisin sauce**

Essentials
1 tablespoon vegetable oil
1 garlic clove, sliced
½ teaspoon salt

Blanch the beans in a large saucepan of lightly salted boiling water for 2 minutes. Drain well.

Heat the oil in a wok or large frying pan, add the garlic and chilli and stir briefly, then add the beans, hoisin sauce and salt. Stir-fry the mixture over a high heat for 1–2 minutes until the beans are tender and well coated with sauce. Serve immediately.

If liked, serve the beans with plain boiled rice or egg noodles.

SESAME CHICKEN KATZU

Serves 2
Preparation time 10 minutes
Cooking time 6—8 minutes

2 skinless **chicken breasts,** each about 175 g (6 oz)

25 g (1 oz) **breadcrumbs**

3 tablespoons **sesame seeds**

Essentials
2 tablespoons plain flour
1 small egg, beaten
3 tablespoons vegetable oil
sweet chilli sauce, for dipping
soy sauce, for dipping

Put the chicken breasts between 2 sheets of clingfilm or nonstick baking paper and flatten with a rolling pin until they are 1 cm (½ inch) thick. Put the flour in one bowl, the egg in a second bowl and the breadcrumbs and sesame seeds in a third. Dip the chicken breasts into the flour, then the egg and finally the breadcrumb and sesame mixture until they are well coated. Press on the breadcrumbs if they fall off.

Heat the oil in a frying pan and fry the chicken for 3—4 minutes on each side until cooked through.Slice the chicken into 2.5 cm (1 inch) strips and serve with sweet chilli sauce and soy sauce as dips.

If liked, serve the chicken with steamed rice or stir-fried vegetables.

MEALS FOR MATES

SAUSAGES & MUSTARD MASH

Serves 4
Preparation time 5 minutes
Cooking time 15 minutes

1 kg (2 lb) **potatoes,** peeled and quartered

8 **pork sausages**

2 **onions,** cut into wedges

1-2 tablespoons **mustard**

Essentials
75 g (3 oz) butter
1 garlic clove, crushed
salt and pepper
dash of olive oil

First start the mash. Put the potatoes into a large saucepan of cold water, bring to the boil and simmer for 15 minutes.

Meanwhile, fry or grill the sausages and the onion wedges over a medium heat for 12-15 minutes, turning the sausages to get an even colour.

Drain the potatoes thoroughly when they are cooked, then mash well so they are smooth and fluffy. Add the butter, mustard, garlic and a good sprinkling of salt and pepper to the potatoes, and carry on mashing. Taste and add more mustard if you want. Finally, stir in a dash of olive oil.

Pile the mash on a plate and serve the sausages and onion wedges on top.

CHICKEN WITH SPRING HERBS

Serves 4
Preparation time 15 minutes
Cooking time 20 minutes

250 g (8 oz) **mascarpone cheese**

bunch of **mixed fresh herbs**, such as chervil, parsley and mint, finely chopped

4 boneless **chicken breasts**, skin on, each about 175 g (6 oz)

200 ml (7 fl oz) **white wine**

Essentials
25 g (1 oz) butter
salt and pepper

Mix together the mascarpone and herbs in a bowl and season well with salt and pepper.

Lift the skin away from each chicken breast and spread a quarter of the mascarpone mixture on each breast. Replace the skin and smooth carefully over the mascarpone mixture. Season to taste with salt and pepper.

Place the chicken in a baking dish and pour the wine around it. Dot the butter over the chicken. Roast in a preheated oven, 180°C (350°F), Gas Mark 4, for 20 minutes until the chicken is golden and crisp. Remove from the oven and serve immediately.

If liked, serve the chicken with garlic bread and a green salad.

ASIAN CHICKEN PARCELS

Serves 4
Preparation time 5 minutes
Cooking time 15 minutes

4 boneless, skinless **chicken breasts**, each
about 250 g (8 oz)

1 tablespoon **clear honey**

2 **red chillies**, deseeded and finely chopped

2.5 cm (1 inch) **fresh root ginger**, peeled
and finely shredded

Essentials
75 ml (3 fl oz) soy
sauce
2 garlic cloves,
sliced

Score the chicken breasts several times with a knife
and put each breast on a piece of kitchen foil 30 cm
(12 inches) square.

Combine the soy sauce, honey, garlic, chillies and
ginger in a small bowl. Spoon the mixture over the
chicken.

Seal the edges of the foil together to form parcels,
transfer to a baking sheet and bake in a preheated
oven, 200°C (400°F), Gas Mark 6, for 15 minutes until
the chicken is cooked through. Leave to rest for 5
minutes, then serve immediately.

If liked, serve the chicken with plain boiled rice.

DOLCELATTE & SPINACH GNOCCHI

Serves 4
Preparation time 5 minutes
Cooking time 20 minutes

500 g (1 lb) ready-made **gnocchi**

125 g (4 oz) **baby spinach**

175 g (6 oz) **dolcelatte cheese**, cubed

125 ml (4 fl oz) **double cream**

Essentials
15 g (½ oz) butter
salt and pepper

Cook the gnocchi in a large saucepan of lightly
salted boiling water according to the instructions
on the packet until they rise to the surface.
Drain thoroughly.

Meanwhile, melt the butter in a saucepan over a high
heat. When it starts to sizzle add the spinach and
cook, stirring, for 1 minute or until just wilted.
Remove from the heat and season to taste with salt
and pepper.

Stir the dolcelatte, cream and drained gnocchi
into the spinach and transfer to an ovenproof dish.
Bake in a preheated oven, 220°C (425°F), Gas Mark 7,
for 12–15 minutes until the sauce is bubbling and
golden.

If liked, scatter 3 tablespoons finely grated
Parmesan cheese over the gnocchi before serving.

ROAST CHICKEN WITH LEMON

Serves 4
Preparation time 15 minutes
Cooking time about 1 hour 40 minutes

1.5 kg (3 lb) **oven-ready chicken**

2 **lemons**

small bunch of **fresh rosemary**, chopped

750 g (1¹/2 lb) **potatoes**, cut into chunks

Essentials
10 garlic cloves
50 g (2 oz) butter
salt and pepper

Put the chicken in a large roasting tin. Finely grate 1 lemon, then cut both lemons into wedges. Crush 2 garlic cloves and set the rest aside. Beat the chopped rosemary, grated lemon rind, crushed garlic, salt and pepper into the butter.

Spread two-thirds of the butter over the chicken and tuck a few lemon wedges inside and on top of the chicken. Loosely cover the chicken with kitchen foil and bake in a preheated oven, 190°C (375°F), Gas Mark 5, for 1 hour.

Remove the foil, spoon over the pan juices and add the potatoes, remaining lemon wedges and garlic to the pan. Roast for 30–40 minutes until the chicken is cooked, turning the potatoes once so that they brown evenly. Spread the chicken with the remaining rosemary butter before serving.

If liked, serve with a green vegetable, such as broccoli or French beans.

CREAMY GARLIC MUSSELS

Serves 4
Preparation time 15 minutes
Cooking time about 8 minutes

1.5 kg (3 lb) fresh, live **mussels**

1 **onion**, finely chopped

100 ml (3¹/₂ fl oz) **white wine**

150 ml (¹/₄ pint) **single cream**

Essentials
15 g (½ oz) butter
6 garlic cloves, finely
   chopped
salt and pepper

Scrub the mussels in cold water, scrape off any barnacles and pull away the dark hairy beards that protrude from the shells. Discard any with broken shells or any open mussels that do not close when tapped sharply.

Melt the butter in a large saucepan, add the onion and garlic and cook for 2—3 minutes until transparent and softened.

Increase the heat and tip in the mussels with the wine. Cover the pan and cook for 3 minutes or until all the shells have opened. Discard any mussels that remain closed.

Pour in the cream and heat through briefly, stirring well. Season well with salt and pepper and serve immediately in large warm bowls.

If liked, serve with crusty bread to mop up the juices and garnish with sprigs of fresh flat leaf parsley.

PESTO TURKEY KEBABS

Serves 4
Preparation time 15 minutes
Cooking time about 12 minutes

4 **turkey breasts**, about 500 g (1 lb) in total
2 tablespoons ready-made **pesto**
4 slices of **Parma ham**
125 g (4 oz) **mozzarella cheese**, cubed

Essentials
1 tablespoon olive oil
salt and pepper

Place a turkey breast between 2 sheets of clingfilm and pound lightly with a mallet until it is about 1 cm (½ inch) thick. Repeat with the remaining turkey breasts.

Spread the pesto over each beaten turkey breast and lay 1 slice of Parma ham on top of each. Sprinkle the mozzarella evenly over the ham, season to taste with salt and pepper and roll up each piece of turkey from the long side.

Cut the turkey rolls into 2.5 cm (1 inch) slices and carefully thread the slices on to 4 metal skewers.

Brush the slices lightly with the oil and grill under a preheated grill for 6 minutes on each side or until cooked through. Increase or reduce the temperature setting of the grill, if necessary, to make sure that the rolls cook through and brown evenly on the outside.

MINTED LAMB SKEWERS

Serves 4
Preparation time 10 minutes
Cooking time 10 minutes

500 g (1 lb) **minced lamb**

6 tablespoons finely chopped **fresh mint leaves**

4 **naan breads**

Essentials
2 teaspoons medium
  curry paste
salt and pepper

Mix together the minced lamb, curry paste and mint in a bowl and season to taste with salt and pepper. Using your hands, knead to combine the mixture evenly.

Divide the mixture into small sausage shapes and thread evenly on to metal skewers. Cook under a preheated grill for 10 minutes, turning once. Serve hot with the warmed naan bread.

If liked, serve the skewers with soured cream and lime wedges or mint raita.

MOROCCAN GRILLED SARDINES

Serves 4
Preparation time 10 minutes
Cooking time 6—8 minutes

12 **sardines**, cleaned and gutted
2 tablespoons **harissa**

Essentials
2 tablespoons olive oil
4 tablespoons lemon juice
salt and pepper

Rinse the sardines and pat them dry with kitchen paper.
Make 3 deep slashes on both sides of each fish with a
sharp knife.

Mix the harissa with the oil and lemon juice to make a
thin paste and rub into both sides of all the sardines.

Transfer the sardines to a lightly oiled baking sheet
and cook under a preheated hot grill for 3—4 minutes
on each side, depending on their size or until cooked
through. Season to taste with salt and pepper and
serve immediately with lemon wedges for squeezing
over, if liked.

DEVILLED CHICKEN

Serves 4
Preparation time 10 minutes
Cooking time 16—20 minutes

8 boneless **chicken thighs**

2 tablespoons **Dijon mustard**

6 drops of **Tabasco sauce**

Essentials
2 garlic cloves, crushed
1 tablespoon soy sauce

Remove the skin from the chicken thighs, open them out and trim away any fat.

Mix together the mustard, Tabasco, garlic and soy sauce in a shallow, non-metallic dish. Dip the trimmed chicken thighs in the sauce, making sure that each piece is well coated.

Heat a large griddle pan or ordinary frying pan. Put the chicken pieces flat on the pan and cook for 8—10 minutes on each side.

If liked, serve the chicken hot with rice or cold with a fresh green salad.

CHICKEN STACKS

Serves 4
Preparation time 10 minutes
Cooking time about 1 hour

4 boneless, skinless **chicken breasts**, each about 125 g (4 oz)

small bunch of **fresh sage**

4 slices of **prosciutto**

4 slices of **fontina cheese**, rind removed

Essentials
olive oil, for drizzling
salt and pepper

Lay the chicken breasts flat on a board and use a sharp knife to slice each one horizontally to give 3 flat pieces.

Heat a griddle pan or ordinary frying pan. Cook 4 pieces of chicken for 5 minutes on each side. When cooked, arrange these on an oiled baking sheet to form the base of the stacks. Put a few sage leaves on top of each one and season to taste with salt and pepper.

Cut each slice of prosciutto in half and cook 4 pieces for 4 minutes on each side. Place these on top of the chicken. Cut each slice of fontina in half. Top each chicken and prosciutto stack with a piece of cheese.

Griddle or fry the remaining chicken and prosciutto and layer as before with the cheese and sage, topping each stack with a piece of chicken. Cook in a preheated oven, 180°C (350°F), Gas Mark 4, for 5–8 minutes or until the cheese is soft.

Drizzle with olive oil, sprinkle with salt and pepper and garnish with the remaining sage leaves.

LIME, GINGER & CORIANDER CHICKEN

Serves 4
Preparation time 5—10 minutes
Cooking time 45-50 minutes

3 limes

1 cm (1/2 inch) cube **fresh root ginger**, peeled and finely grated

4 tablespoons finely chopped **fresh coriander**, plus extra leaves to serve

4 chicken legs

Essentials
2 teaspoons vegetable oil
salt

Finely grate the rind of 2 of the limes and halve these limes. Mix the rind with the ginger and coriander in a non-metallic bowl and stir in 1 teaspoon oil to make a rough paste.

Carefully lift the skin from the chicken legs and push the ginger paste under the skin. Smooth the skin back into place, then cut 3—4 slashes in the thickest parts of the legs and brush with the remaining oil.

Put the chicken in a roasting tin, flesh side down, with the halved limes and cook in a preheated oven, 220°C (425°F), Gas Mark 7, for 45—50 minutes, basting occasionally. The legs are cooked when the meat comes away from the bone and the juices run clear.

Place the chicken legs on a plate, squeeze over the roasted lime and scatter with coriander leaves. Serve immediately with the remaining lime, cut into wedges.

If liked, serve the chicken with plain boiled rice and a green vegetable.

LEMON CHILLI CHICKEN

Serves 4
Preparation time 25 minutes, plus marinating
Cooking time 45 minutes

1.75 kg (3¹/2 lb) **chicken**, cut into 8 pieces

4 juicy **lemons**

1 small **red chilli**, deseeded and chopped

2 teaspoons **clear honey**

Essentials
8 garlic cloves
4 tablespoons dried parsley
salt and pepper

Arrange the chicken pieces in a shallow, non-metallic flameproof dish. Squeeze the juice from the lemons and reserve the skins.

Peel and crush 2 of the garlic cloves and mix them with the lemon juice, chilli and honey. Stir well and pour this mixture over the chicken. Tuck the lemon skins around the meat, cover and leave to marinate in the refrigerator for at least 2 hours or overnight, turning once or twice.

Arrange the chicken pieces so they are skin side up, scatter over the remaining garlic and put the lemon skins, cut sides down, on top.

Cook the chicken in a preheated oven, 200°C (400°F), Gas Mark 6, for 45 minutes or until golden-brown and tender. Stir in the parsley, season to taste and serve immediately.

If liked, garnish the chicken with sprigs of fresh parsley before serving.

DEEP-FRIED POLLOCK

Serves 4
Preparation time 15 minutes
Cooking time 20 minutes

1 tablespoon **cornflour**

2 tablespoons chopped **fresh coriander**

125 ml (4 fl oz) **sparkling water**

425 g (14 oz) **pollock fillet,** pin-boned and cut into 8 x 2.5 cm (3 x 1 inch) strips

Essentials
150 g (5 oz) self-raising flour
vegetable oil, for deep-frying
sweet chilli sauce, for dipping
salt and pepper

Put the flour, cornflour, coriander and a good pinch of salt and pepper in a large bowl. Using a fork, stir in the sparkling water to make a batter the consistency of double cream. Do not overstir the batter; it does not matter if there are small lumps of flour. Pat the fish strips dry on kitchen paper and dip them into the batter.

Pour the oil into a deep-fat fryer or into a large saucepan to a depth of at least 8 cm (3 inches) and heat to 180–190°C (350–375°F) or until a cube of bread browns in 30 seconds. Cook the fish in small batches until it is golden-brown. Drain on kitchen paper and keep warm while you cook the remainder.

Serve the fish goujons hot with some sweet chilli sauce for dipping.

LAMB HOTPOT

Serves 4
Preparation time 20 minutes
Cooking time 2¼ hours

8 **lamb chops,** about 1 kg (2 lb) in total

2 **onions,** sliced

200 g (7 oz) **chestnut mushrooms,** halved

1 kg (2 lb) large **potatoes,** thinly sliced

Essentials
50 g (2 oz) butter
1 tablespoon oil
2 teaspoons dried rosemary
4 garlic cloves, sliced
450 ml (¾ pint) lamb stock
salt and pepper

Trim away any excess fat from the lamb and season the meat lightly on both sides with salt and pepper. Melt half the butter with the oil in a shallow, flameproof casserole and fry the lamb in batches until browned. Drain to a plate.

Return the lamb to the casserole, arranging them side by side, and sprinkle with the rosemary and garlic. Tuck the onions and mushrooms around them, then place the potatoes on top. Pour the stock over. Cover with a lid or kitchen foil and bake in a preheated oven, 160°C (325°F), Gas Mark 3, for 1½ hours. Dot with the remaining butter, return to the oven and cook, uncovered, for a further 45 minutes or until the potato topping is crisped and browned.

FINGER-LICKING GARLIC PRAWNS

Serves 4
Preparation time 15 minutes
Cooking time about 4 minutes

24 raw **tiger prawns**, peeled

1 tablespoon chopped **fresh parsley**

Essentials
100 g (3½ oz) butter
2 garlic cloves, crushed
2 tablespoons lemon juice
salt and pepper

Devein the prawns by cutting down the back of each
one with a sharp knife and removing the black cord.
Melt the butter in a large frying pan, add the garlic
and fry gently for 30 seconds. Add the prawns, season
to taste with salt and pepper and cook over a low
heat for about 3 minutes or until the prawns are just
cooked through, turning them once.

Remove the pan from the heat and stir in the parsley
and lemon juice.

Allow the prawns to cool slightly before serving them
with crusty bread to mop up the juices, if liked.

TUNA ENCHILADAS

Serves 4
Preparation time 10 minutes
Cooking time 15 minutes

2 ripe **tomatoes**, roughly chopped
1 **onion**, finely chopped
8 **chapattis**

300 g (10 oz) can **tuna** in olive oil, drained

Essentials
1 tablespoon lemon juice
 (to taste)
salt and pepper

Mix together the tomatoes and onion. Season well
with salt and pepper and add lemon juice to taste.

Spoon some of the tomato mixture over each chapatti
and top with tuna. Roll up each chapatti and arrange
them in a heatproof dish. Sprinkle over any
remaining tomato salsa.

Cover and cook in a preheated oven, 200°C (400°F),
Gas Mark 6, for 15 minutes until golden. Serve
immediately.

If liked, scatter 75 g (3 oz) grated Cheddar cheese
over the chapattis before baking.

BAKED CHEESE FONDUE

Serves 4
Preparation time 5 minutes
Cooking time 12—15 minutes

1 whole **Camembert cheese**, about 200 g (7 oz)

2 teaspoons chopped **fresh thyme leaves,** plus a few extra to garnish

1 **baguette,** sliced

250 g (8 oz) **cherry tomatoes**

Essentials
1 tablespoon olive oil
salt and pepper

Put the Camembert on a foil-lined baking sheet. Drizzle over the oil, scatter over the chopped thyme and season with salt and pepper.

Bake in a preheated oven, 200°C (400°F), Gas Mark 6, for 12—15 minutes until the cheese is sizzling and ready to burst through the skin.

Carefully transfer the cheese to a platter and serve with the sliced bread and tomatoes to dip into the oozing cheese.

HEALTHY FIXES

PEAR, KIWIFRUIT & LIME JUICE

Makes 300 ml (½ pint)
Preparation time 5 minutes

3 **kiwifruit**, plus extra to serve (optional)

2 ripe **pears**

1/2 **lime**

2–3 **ice cubes** (optional)

Peel and slice the kiwifruit. Cut the pears and lime into evenly sized pieces. Juice the fruit.

Pour the juice into a tall glass, add a couple of ice cubes (if used), decorate with slices of kiwifruit, if liked, and serve immediately.

BEETROOT & BERRY SMOOTHIE

Makes 250 ml (8 fl oz)
Preparation time 5 minutes

50 g (2 oz) **beetroot**

100 g (3¹/2 oz) **blueberries**, plus extra
to serve (optional)

100 g (3¹/2 oz) **raspberries**

2–3 **ice cubes**

Juice the beetroot. Pour the beetroot juice into a
food processor or blender, add the blueberries,
raspberries and ice cubes and process until smooth.

Pour the mixture into a glass, decorate with
blueberries, if liked, and serve immediately.

TROPICAL JUICE

Makes 300 ml (½ pint)
Preparation time 5 minutes

1 **mango**

2 **passionfruit**

3 **apples**, preferably red, plus extra
to serve (optional)

ice cubes

Peel the mango and remove the stone. Slice the
passionfruit in half, scoop out the flesh and
discard the seeds. Juice the apples with the mango
and passionfruit.

Pour the juice into a tall glass over ice, decorate
with apple slices, if liked, and serve immediately.

EXOTIC FRUIT SALAD

Serves 6–8
Preparation time 10 minutes

1 large ripe **pineapple**, about 1.5 kg (3 lb)

1 **papaya**, about 400 g (13 oz)

3 **passionfruit**

2–3 tablespoons **lime juice**

Peel and core the pineapple and cut the flesh into small wedges. Do the same with the papaya, carefully removing the seeds with a spoon. Put the pineapple and papaya in a serving bowl.

Cut the passionfruit in half and scrape the pulp into the bowl. Add the lime juice, mix carefully and serve.

STRAWBERRY CRUSH

Serves 2

Preparation time 10 minutes

200 g (7 oz) **strawberries**

1 tablespoon **icing sugar**, plus extra for dusting

200 ml (7 fl oz) **Greek yogurt**

2 ready-made **meringue nests**

Reserve 4 small strawberries for decoration. Hull
the remainder, put them in a bowl with the sugar and
mash together with a fork. Alternatively, process
the strawberries and sugar in a food processor or
blender to a smooth purée.

Put the yogurt in a bowl, crumble in the meringues
and lightly mix together. Add the strawberry purée
and fold together with a spoon until marbled. Spoon
into 2 dessert glasses or glass bowls.

Cut the reserved strawberries in half and arrange
them on top of the strawberry crush. Lightly dust
with icing sugar and serve immediately.

FIG & HONEY POTS

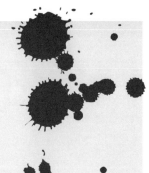

Serves 2
Preparation time 10 minutes, plus chilling

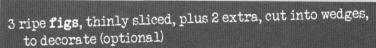

3 ripe **figs**, thinly sliced, plus 2 extra, cut into wedges, to decorate (optional)

225 ml (7 1/2 fl oz) **Greek yogurt**

2 tablespoons **clear honey**

1 tablespoon chopped **pistachio nuts**

Arrange the fig slices snugly in the bottom of 2 dessert glasses or glass bowls. Spoon the yogurt over the figs and chill in the refrigerator for 10—15 minutes.

Just before serving, drizzle honey over each bowl and sprinkle the pistachio nuts on top. Decorate with the wedges of fig, if liked.

MIXED BERRY SALAD

Serves 2
Preparation time 10 minutes

200 g (7 oz) **strawberries**

75 g (3 oz) **blueberries**

small bunch of **fresh mint**, finely chopped, a few sprigs reserved for decoration

1–2 tablespoons **elderflower syrup** (to taste)

Hull and halve the strawberries. Wash all the berries and drain well.

Add the chopped mint to the berries with the elderflower syrup, mix carefully and serve, decorated with the reserved mint sprigs.

CHARGRILLED FRUIT WITH CHILLI SALT

Serves 6—8
Preparation time 15 minutes
Cooking time 10 minutes

1 large **mango**, peeled and stoned

1/2 **pineapple**, peeled

2 **bananas**

Essentials
1 tablespoon salt
½ teaspoon dried chilli
  flakes, crushed

Mix together the chilli and salt and set aside.
Cut the mango into 2 cm (¾ inch) pieces and cut
the pineapple into small wedges. Cut the bananas
into thick slices. Skewer the fruit on to metal or
presoaked wooden skewers, alternating the fruits.

Preheat a griddle pan or grill to medium heat and
grill the skewers on each side for 3 minutes until
golden and caramelized. Remove the skewers from the
heat, sprinkle with the salt chilli mix and serve.

SUMMER GREEN PEA SOUP

Serves 2
Preparation time 10 minutes
Cooking time about 15 minutes

bunch of **spring onions**, chopped

250 g (8 oz) frozen **peas**

1 tablespoon thick **natural yogurt** or **single cream**

1 tablespoon chopped and 2 whole **chives**, to garnish

Essentials
5 g (¼ oz) butter
375 ml (13 fl oz) vegetable stock
nutmeg

Melt the butter in a large pan. Add the onions and cook gently until they are softened but do not allow them to colour. Add the peas to the pan with the stock. Bring to the boil and simmer for about 5 minutes or until they are cooked.

Remove from the heat and purée in a food processor or blender. Add the yogurt or cream and grate in a little nutmeg. Reheat gently if necessary and serve sprinkled with chives.

CARROT & GINGER SOUP

Serves 2
Preparation time 20 minutes
Cooking time 25–30 minutes

1 small **onion**, chopped

1–2 teaspoons finely grated
fresh root ginger (to taste)

175 g (6 oz) **carrots**, sliced

Essentials
1 tablespoon olive oil
1 garlic clove, crushed
450 ml (¾ pint) vegetable
  or chicken stock
1 tablespoon lemon juice
salt and pepper

Heat the oil in a saucepan. Add the onion, garlic
and ginger and cook over a low heat for 5–6 minutes
or until softened.

Add the carrots and stock and bring to the boil.
Reduce the heat and simmer for 15–20 minutes or
until the carrots are tender.

Purée the soup in a food processor or blender with
the lemon juice until smooth. Strain through a sieve
and return to the saucepan to reheat.

If liked, serve the soup with a spoonful of soured
cream in each bowl and a sprinkling of finely
chopped spring onions.

CALDO VERDE

Serves 2
Preparation time 15 minutes
Cooking time 35 minutes

50 g (2 oz) dark green **cabbage,** such as Cavolo Nero
1 small **onion,** chopped
300 g (10 oz) floury **potatoes,** cut into small chunks
200 g (7 oz) can **cannellini beans,** drained

Essentials
2 tablespoons olive oil
1 garlic clove, chopped
500 ml (17 fl oz) vegetable stock
2 teaspoons dried coriander
salt and pepper

Discard any tough stalk ends from the cabbage and roll the leaves up tightly. Use a large knife to shred the cabbage as finely as possible.

Heat the oil in a large saucepan. Add the onion and fry gently for 5 minutes. Add the potatoes and cook, stirring occasionally, for 10 minutes. Stir in the garlic and cook for a further 1 minute.

Add the stock and bring to the boil. Reduce the heat and simmer gently, covered, for about 10 minutes until the potatoes are tender. Use a potato masher to lightly mash the potatoes into the soup so that they are broken up but not completely puréed.

Stir in the beans, shredded cabbage and coriander and cook gently for a further 10 minutes. Season to taste with salt and pepper.

CHICKPEA TAGINE

Serves 2
Preparation time 15 minutes
Cooking time 30-35 minutes

1 small **onion**, finely chopped

1 small **aubergine**, about 175 g (6 oz), diced

200 g (7 oz) can **chickpeas**, drained

200 g (7 oz) can **chopped tomatoes**

Essentials

4 tablespoons olive oil
1 garlic clove, crushed
1 teaspoon ground coriander
½ teaspoon each ground cumin, ground turmeric and ground cinnamon
150 ml (¼ pint) vegetable stock
salt and pepper

Heat 2 tablespoons oil in a saucepan. Add the onion, garlic and spices and cook over a medium heat, stirring frequently, for 5 minutes until lightly golden.

Heat a further 2 tablespoons oil in the pan, add the aubergines and cook, stirring, for 4—5 minutes until browned. Add the chickpeas, tomatoes and stock and bring to the boil.

Reduce the heat, cover and simmer gently for 20—25 minutes. Season to taste with salt and pepper.

Serve with couscous, if liked.

ASIAN CITRUS CHICKEN SKEWERS

Serves 2
Preparation time 5 minutes, plus marinating
Cooking time 20 minutes

250 g (8 oz) boneless, skinless **chicken breasts**, cubed

grated rind and juice of
1/2 **lemon**

1 teaspoon Chinese **5 spice powder**

Essentials
2–3 teaspoons soy sauce
  (to taste)

Put the chicken, lemon rind and juice, 5 spice powder and soy sauce in a bowl. Stir to combine, cover, then leave to marinate in the refrigerator for at least 1 hour or overnight.

Thread the chicken pieces on to 2 metal or presoaked wooden skewers, pushing them tightly together. Grill for 10 minutes under a preheated moderate grill. Turn the skewers, baste with any remaining marinade, and grill for a further 10 minutes.

If liked, serve the skewers on a bed of mixed vegetables.

SMOKED MACKEREL KEDGEREE

Serves 2
Preparation time 5 minutes
Cooking time about 10 minutes

175 g (6 oz) **smoked mackerel**, flaked

175 g (6 oz) cooked **basmati rice**

1/2-1 teaspoon **mild curry paste** (to taste)

2 tablespoons chopped **fresh parsley**

Essentials
2 eggs
15 g (½ oz) butter
2 tablespoons lemon juice

Put the eggs in a small pan of boiling water and cook for 7 minutes. Drain, run under cold water, peel and cut into quarters.

Meanwhile, heat the butter in a frying pan, add the mackerel, rice and curry paste and toss until everything is warmed through and the rice is evenly coated.

Stir in the lemon juice, parsley and boiled eggs and serve immediately.

LEBANESE LENTIL & BULGAR SALAD

Serves 2
Preparation time 10 minutes
Cooking time 30 minutes

50 g (2 oz) **Puy lentils**

50 g (2 oz) **bulgar wheat**

1 **onion**, sliced

handful of **fresh mint**, chopped

Essentials

2 teaspoons tomato purée
375 ml (13 fl oz) vegetable
  stock
2 tablespoons lemon juice
2 teaspoons olive oil
½ teaspoon sugar
salt and pepper

Put the lentils, tomato purée and stock in a saucepan and bring to the boil. Reduce the heat, cover tightly and simmer for 20 minutes. Add the bulgar wheat and lemon juice and season to taste with salt and pepper. Cook for 10 minutes until all the stock has been absorbed.

Meanwhile, heat the oil in a frying pan, add the onions and sugar and cook over a low heat until deep brown and caramelized.

Stir the mint into the lentil and bulgar wheat mixture, then serve warm, topped with the fried caramelized onions.

PRAWN, MANGO & AVOCADO SALAD

Serves 2
Preparation time 10 minutes

about 225 g (7½ oz) **mango** flesh

about 200 g (7 oz) **avocado** flesh

1 **cos lettuce**

8 large cooked **king prawns**, peeled but tails left on

Essentials
2 tablespoons lemon juice
½ teaspoon sugar
1 tablespoon vegetable oil
1—2 teaspoons dried chilli flakes (to taste)

Cut the mango and avocado flesh into 2 cm (¾ inch) pieces. Discard the outer layer of leaves and cut the stems off the lettuce, leaving the hearts. Separate the leaves and add them to the mango and avocado with the prawns.

Whisk together the lemon juice, sugar and oil with the chilli flakes. Add the dressing to the salad, toss carefully to mix and serve immediately.

CAESAR SALAD

Serves 2-3
Preparation time 20 minutes

1 cos lettuce

25 g (1 oz) **anchovy fillets** in olive oil

50 g (2 oz) ready-made **croutons**

75 ml (3 fl oz) ready-made **Caesar dressing**

Essentials
salt and pepper

Tear the lettuce leaves into bite-sized pieces and put them in a salad bowl.

Drain the anchovies, chop them into small pieces and scatter them over the lettuce. Mix the croutons into the salad.

Pour the dressing over the salad and mix gently to combine.

If liked, scatter Parmesan shavings over the salad before serving.

POTATO SALAD

Serves 2–3
Preparation time 10 minutes, plus cooling
Cooking time 15 minutes

500 g (1 lb) **new potatoes**

50 g (2 oz) **smoked streaky bacon**

3 **spring onions**

75 ml (3 fl oz) ready-made **mayonnaise**

Essentials
1 teaspoon vegetable oil
salt and pepper

Halve the potatoes and cook them in lightly salted boiling water until tender. Rinse under cold water and leave to cool.

Meanwhile, cut the bacon into thin strips. Heat the oil in a frying pan. Add the bacon and cook until golden. Drain on kitchen paper and allow to cool. Finely slice the spring onions, reserving some for a garnish.

Put the potatoes, sliced spring onions and bacon in a large salad bowl. Gently stir in the mayonnaise. Season to taste with salt and pepper, garnish with the reserved spring onions and serve.

TV DINNERS & SNACKS

POTATO WEDGES

Serves 2
Preparation time 20 minutes
Cooking time 30—35 minutes

1 **sweet potato**, skin on

1 large **baking potato**, skin on

1/2 teaspoon **Cajun spice**

1 tablespoon chopped **fresh parsley**

Essentials
2 tablespoons olive oil

Cut the sweet potato in half, cut each half into
4 wedges and put the pieces in a large mixing bowl.
Cut the baking potato in half, cut each half into
6 thick wedges and add them to the bowl. Drizzle
over the oil and toss well to coat.

Transfer the potatoes to a large baking sheet and
arrange them in a single layer. Sprinkle over the
Cajun spice and roast in a preheated oven, 200°C
(400°F), Gas Mark 6, for 30—35 minutes until golden
and cooked through.

Turn on to a warm serving platter and sprinkle with
the parsley.

If liked, serve the wedges with mayonnaise or a
dip made from 4 tablespoons Greek yogurt mixed with
2 tablespoons soured cream, 2 tablespoons chopped
chives and 1 tablespoon grated Parmesan cheese.

LIGHTLY SPICED CHICKEN NUGGETS

Serves 2
Preparation time 15 minutes
Cooking time 15—20 minutes

2 boneless, skinless **chicken breasts**, each about 150 g (5 oz), cut into bite-sized pieces

150 g (5 oz) fine **wholemeal breadcrumbs**

1 teaspoon **Cajun spice**

2 tablespoons chopped **fresh parsley**

Essentials
25 g (1 oz) plain flour
1 small egg, beaten

Put the flour in a shallow bowl and toss the chicken in it so the meat is evenly coated.

Pour the beaten egg on to a saucer. Mix the breadcrumbs with the Cajun spice and parsley on a separate plate. Dip each of the chicken pieces in the beaten egg, then toss in the seasoned breadcrumbs. Transfer to a large baking sheet.

Roast the chicken in a preheated oven, 200°C (400°F), Gas Mark 6, for 15—20 minutes until golden and cooked through. Serve immediately.

If liked, serve with tomato ketchup to dip.

MINI BEEF AND BEAN BURGERS

Makes 4 burgers
Preparation time 15 minutes
Cooking time 10 minutes

125 g (4 oz) can **red kidney beans**, rinsed and drained

1/2 small **onion**, finely chopped

200 g (7 oz) lean **minced beef**

Essentials
½ teaspoon coriander seeds
½ teaspoon cumin seeds
½ teaspoon ground paprika
vegetable oil, for frying

Put the beans in a bowl and mash them with a fork to break them into small pieces. Add the onion and beef.

Roughly crush the coriander and cumin seeds with a pestle and mortar or use a small bowl and the end of a rolling pin to crush the seeds. Add to the bowl together with the paprika and mix well with your hands.

Turn the mixture out on a board and divide it into 4 portions. Shape each piece into a ball with your hands and flatten it to make a burger.

Heat a thin layer of oil in a large frying pan and gently fry the burgers for 5 minutes on each side until they are well browned. Transfer to warm serving plates and serve immediately.

Serve with a green salad and, if liked, tomato ketchup or mayonnaise.

POTATO & CHEESE BURGERS

Makes 4 burgers
Preparation time 10 minutes
Cooking time 20 minutes

500 g (1 lb) red or waxy **potatoes**

150 g (5 oz) mild **Cheddar cheese**, grated

1 small **red onion**, finely chopped

Essentials
vegetable oil, for frying
salt and pepper

Put the potatoes in a large pan of lightly salted water and bring to the boil. Boil for about 20 minutes until the potatoes are just cooked but firm. Drain and cool.

Peel the potatoes and grate them into a bowl. Stir in the cheese and onion and season to taste with salt and pepper. Divide the mixture into 4 and shape each portion into a ball with your hands and flatten it to make a burger.

Heat a thin layer of oil in a large frying pan and gently fry the burgers over a medium heat for 4—5 minutes on each side. Eat the burgers hot or cold.

TUNA FISH CAKES

Makes 6 small cakes
Preparation time 10 minutes
Cooking time 10 minutes

425 g (14 oz) can **tuna** in olive oil, drained

150 g (5 oz) **ricotta cheese**

3 **spring onions**, finely chopped

grated rind of 1 **lime**

Essentials
1 egg, beaten
1½ tablespoons olive
  oil
salt and pepper

Flake the tuna into a bowl and use a wooden spoon to mix in the ricotta, spring onions, lime rind and egg. Season to taste with salt and pepper.

Divide the mixture into 6 and shape each portion into a ball with your hands. Flatten it to make small cakes about 8 cm (3 inches) across.

Heat the oil in a frying pan, add the fish cakes and cook over a medium heat for 4–5 minutes on each side until golden.

If liked, serve with a salad of rocket leaves with a dressing made from equal parts of olive oil and lime juice.

SEARED CHICKEN SANDWICH

Serves 2
Preparation time 15 mi5nutes
Cooking time 5—6 minutes

125 g (4 oz) mini **chicken breast** fillets

4 slices of **bread**

3 tablespoons **natural yogurt**

50 g (2 oz) **mixed salad leaves**

Essentials
4 teaspoons balsamic vinegar
pepper

Put the chicken in a plastic bag with half the vinegar and toss together until evenly coated. Heat a nonstick frying pan, lift the chicken out of the plastic bag with a fork and add the pieces to the pan. Fry for 3 minutes, turn and drizzle with the vinegar from the bag and cook for 2—3 more minutes or until browned and cooked through.

Meanwhile, toast the bread lightly on both sides. Cut the cooked chicken into long, thin strips and arrange them on 2 slices of toast. Season the yogurt with a little pepper to taste. Add the salad leaves and toss together.

Spoon the yogurt and salad leaves over the chicken, drizzle over the remaining vinegar, if liked, and top with the remaining slices of toast. Cut each sandwich in half and serve immediately.

THAI CHILLI BEEF BURGERS

Makes 4 small burgers
Preparation time 10 minutes
Cooking time 10 minutes

250 g (8 oz) **minced beef**

1–2 teaspoons **Thai red curry paste** (to taste)

25 g (1 oz) fresh **white breadcrumbs**

Essentials
1 egg, lightly beaten
1 tablespoon soy sauce
pepper

Put the beef in a bowl and stir in the curry paste, breadcrumbs, egg, soy sauce and pepper. Mix together thoroughly with your hands until the mixture is sticky. Shape the mixture into 4 and shape each portion into a ball with your hands. Flatten to make small burgers.

Heat a ridged griddle pan or nonstick frying pan until very hot, add the burgers and cook over a high heat for 4–5 minutes on each side until charred and cooked through. Serve immediately.

If liked, serve each burger on a slice of French bread with some sweet chilli sauce on the side.

AUBERGINE DIP

Serves 2
Preparation time 15 minutes, plus cooling
Cooking time 15 minutes

1 small **aubergine**

50 ml (2 fl oz) **Greek yogurt**

1 tablespoon chopped **fresh coriander**

2 **flour tortillas**

Essentials
2 tablespoons olive oil
½ teaspoon ground cumin
1 small garlic clove, crushed
½ tablespoon lemon juice
salt and pepper

Cut the aubergine lengthways into 5 mm (¼ inch) thick slices. Mix 1 tablespoon oil with the cumin and salt and pepper and brush all over the aubergine slices.

Cook in a preheated ridged griddle pan or under a preheated hot grill for 3—4 minutes on each side until charred and tender. Leave to cool, then chop finely.

Put the yogurt in a bowl. Add the chopped aubergine and stir in the garlic, coriander, lemon juice and the remaining oil. Season to taste with salt and pepper and transfer to a serving bowl.

Serve the dip with flour tortillas cooked in a preheated griddle pan or under the hot grill for 3 minutes on each side and then cut into triangles.

CHICKEN & HUMMUS WRAPS

Serves 2
Preparation time 5 minutes
Cooking time 10 minutes

3 boneless, skinless **chicken thighs,** about 250 g (8 oz) in total

2 flour tortillas

100 g (3 1/2 oz) **hummus**

25 g (1 oz) **rocket** or **salad leaves**

Essentials
1 tablespoon olive oil
1 small garlic clove, crushed
½ teaspoon ground cumin
salt and pepper

Cut the chicken thighs into quarters and put them in a bowl. Combine the oil, garlic and cumin and season to taste with salt and pepper. Add to the bowl with the chicken and stir well.

Heat a ridged griddle pan or nonstick frying pan until hot. Thread the chicken pieces on to metal skewers, add to the pan and cook for 4—5 minutes on each side. Remove and leave to rest for 5 minutes.

Meanwhile, warm the tortillas in a preheated oven, 150°C (350°F), Gas Mark 2, for 5 minutes.

Remove the chicken from the skewers. Divide the hummus, rocket or salad leaves and chicken between the tortillas. Wrap and serve immediately.

JERK CHICKEN WINGS

Serves 2
Preparation time 5 minutes, plus marinating
Cooking time 12 minutes

6 large **chicken wings**

1/2 tablespoon **jerk seasoning mix**

Essentials
1 tablespoon olive oil
1 tablespoon lemon juice
½ teaspoon salt

Put the chicken wings in a non-metallic dish. Put the oil in a small bowl and whisk it with the lemon juice, salt and jerk seasoning. Pour the mixture over the chicken and stir well until evenly coated. Cover and leave to marinate in the refrigerator for at least 30 minutes or overnight.

Arrange the chicken wings on a grill rack and cook under a preheated grill, basting halfway through cooking with any remaining marinade, for 6 minutes on each side or until cooked through, tender and lightly charred at the edges. Increase or reduce the temperature setting of the grill if necessary to make sure that the wings cook through. Serve immediately with lemon wedges for squeezing over, if liked.

CHICKEN TACOS

Serves 2
Preparation time 10 minutes
Cooking time 16–20 minutes

2 boneless, skinless **chicken breasts,**
each about 175 g (6 oz)

125 ml (1/4 pint) ready-made
tomato salsa

8 **taco shells**

75 ml (3 fl oz) **soured cream**

Essentials
1 tablespoon vegetable oil

Heat a griddle pan or ordinary frying pan. Brush the
chicken breasts with oil, put them in the pan and
cook for 8–10 minutes on each side. Remove from the
pan and slice into strips.

Spoon some salsa into each taco shell and top with
a few strips of chicken. Serve the remaining salsa
separately, with a bowl of soured cream to spoon on
top of the tacos just before eating.

CHICKEN SATAY

Serves 2
Preparation time 10 minutes, plus marinating
Cooking time 10 minutes

1 tablespoon smooth **peanut butter**

50 ml (2 fl oz) **lime juice**

1/2 teaspoon **hot pepper sauce**

2 boneless, skinless **chicken breasts**, each about 175 g (6 oz), cubed

Essentials
50 ml (2 fl oz) soy sauce
15 g (½ oz) medium curry
  paste
1 garlic clove, chopped

Combine the peanut butter, soy sauce, lime juice, curry paste, garlic and hot pepper sauce in a non-metallic dish. Add the chicken, mix well and chill for 12 hours or until required.

When ready to serve, thread the chicken cubes on metal skewers and cook under a preheated hot grill for 5 minutes on each side until tender and cooked through. Serve immediately.

If liked, serve with lemon wedges and chunks of cucumber and onion.

BAKED SWEET POTATOES

Serves 2
Preparation time 5 minutes
Cooking time 45–50 minutes

2 **sweet potatoes**, each about 250 g (8 oz)

100 g (3¹/2 oz) **soured cream**

1 **spring onion**, trimmed and finely chopped

1/2 tablespoon chopped **fresh chives**

Essentials
25 g (1 oz) butter
salt and pepper

Scrub the potatoes, put them in a roasting tin and roast in a preheated oven, 220°C (425°F), Gas Mark 7, for 45–50 minutes until cooked through.

Meanwhile, combine the soured cream, spring onion and chives in a bowl. Season to taste with salt and pepper.

Cut the baked potatoes in half lengthways, top with butter and spoon over the soured cream mixture. Serve immediately.

HEALTHY SPICED CHIPS

Serves 2
Preparation time 15 minutes
Cooking time about 45 minutes

4 potatoes, each about 150 g (5 oz)

Essentials
1 egg white
½ teaspoon paprika
pinch of cayenne pepper
olive oil, for greasing
salt and pepper

Cut the potatoes into chunky wedges and put them in a bowl. Lightly whisk the egg white until frothy and stir into the potato wedges so they are evenly coated. Add the spices and plenty of salt and pepper and toss together so that the wedges are lightly coated with seasoning.

Arrange the wedges in a single layer on a baking sheet lined with nonstick baking paper and brushed with oil. Cook in a preheated oven, 230°C (450°F), Gas Mark 8, for about 45 minutes, turning a couple of times until golden. Serve immediately.

If liked, serve the potato wedges with tomato ketchup, mayonnaise or tomato salsa.

BRUNCH CROQUE MONSIEUR

Serves 2
Preparation time 8 minutes
Cooking time 4–5 minutes

4 thick slices of **French country bread**

50 g (2 oz) finely grated
Parmesan cheese

2 large slices of country-style **roast ham**

100 g (3 1/2 oz) **Emmental cheese**, coarsely grated

Essentials
30 g (1¼ oz) butter, melted

Brush one side of each slice of bread with melted butter and sprinkle with the Parmesan.

So that the Parmesan-coated sides are on the outside, lay 2 slices of bread on a plate and top each with a slice of ham and half the coarsely grated Emmental.

Top with the remaining two slices of bread and toast in a sandwich grill for 4—5 minutes or according to the manufacturer's instructions until the bread is golden and crispy and the Emmental is beginning to ooze from the sides. Serve immediately.

Top each sandwich with a fried egg if you want to make a brunch croque madame.

PASTRAMI WITH RED ONION CHUTNEY

Serves 2
Preparation time 8 minutes
Cooking time 3–4 minutes

4 slices of **rye bread**

4 tablespoons **onion chutney**

150 g (5 oz) shaved **pastrami**

2 slices of mature **Cheddar cheese**

Place 2 slices of bread on a plate and spoon chutney over each slice. Add a layer of shaved pastrami on top.

Put the slices of Cheddar on the pastrami and top with the lids. Toast in a sandwich grill for 3—4 minutes or according to the manufacturer's instructions until the bread is toasted and the cheese has melted. Serve immediately.

Serve with barbecue sauce, if liked.

TUNA, PESTO & MOZZARELLA CIABATTA

Serves 2
Preparation time 5 minutes
Cooking time 4—5 minutes

4 tablespoons ready-made **red pesto sauce**

2 large **ciabatta rolls**, cut in half horizontally

150 g (5 oz) can **tuna** in olive oil, drained

50 g (2 oz) **mozzarella cheese**, thinly sliced

Essentials
2 teaspoons olive oil
1 teaspoon balsamic vinegar
1—2 teaspoons dried basil

Spread the pesto evenly over each ciabatta base. Top with the tuna and the mozzarella slices. Drizzle the oil and balsamic vinegar over them and finish with the basil.

Top with the lids and toast in a sandwich grill for 4—5 minutes or according to the manufacturer's instructions until they are golden and crispy. Serve immediately.

AUBERGINE & MOZZARELLA PANINI

Serves 2—4
Preparation time 10 minutes
Cooking time 10—15 minutes

1 large **aubergine**, sliced widthways into
5 mm (1/4 inch) slices
1 **ciabatta**
2 tablespoons **olive tapenade**
250 g (8 oz) **mozzarella cheese**, thinly sliced

Essentials
1 tablespoon olive
oil
vegetable oil, for
frying
salt and pepper

Brush the aubergine slices with the olive oil and season
lightly with salt and pepper. Heat a ridged griddle pan until
hot. Add the aubergine slices, in batches if necessary, and
cook for 3—4 minutes on each side until charred and tender.
Remove and set aside. Clean the griddle pan.

Cut the ciabatta into quarters, then trim the quarters so
that all 4 pieces will fit in the griddle pan. Heat the
griddle pan and brush with a little vegetable oil. Add the
ciabatta pieces, cut side down, and cook for 1 minute, or
until toasted and charred. Depending on the size of your
griddle pan, you may have to toast the bread in batches.
Spread the toasted sides of the ciabatta with the tapenade
and sandwich together with layers of mozzarella and
aubergine slices.

Add the whole sandwiches to the griddle pan and cook for
1—2 minutes on each side until toasted and the cheese in
the centre has melted. Serve immediately.

If liked, serve with a green salad.

TOFFEE & CHOCOLATE POPCORN

Serves 2
Preparation time 1 minute
Cooking time 4 minutes

25 g (1 oz) **popping corn**

125 g (4 oz) **light muscovado sugar**

1 tablespoon **cocoa powder**

Essentials
150 g (5 oz) butter

Put the popping corn in a large bowl with a lid and microwave on high (900 watts) for 4 minutes.

Alternatively, cook in a pan with a lid on the hob, over a medium heat, for a few minutes until popping. Meanwhile, gently heat the butter, sugar and cocoa powder in a pan until the sugar has dissolved and the butter has melted.

Stir the warm popcorn into the mixture and serve.

MULTICOLOURED FRESH FRUIT LOLLIES

Makes 8 lollies
Preparation time 20 minutes, plus freezing
Cooking time 15 minutes

300 g (10 oz) **raspberries**

400 g (13 oz) can **peaches** in natural juice

Essentials
25 g (1 oz) caster sugar

Put the raspberries and sugar in a small pan with 4 tablespoons water and bring to the boil, stirring well until the sugar has dissolve. Add a further 150 ml (¼ pint) water.

Press the raspberry liquid through a sieve, pushing down well with a metal spoon to make as much of the pulp go through as possible. Discard the seeds. Pour the mixture into 8 lolly moulds, filling just the base of each. (You could use 8 clean, small yogurt pots placed in a roasting tin. Cover with foil and push lolly sticks through the foil into the centre of each pot. The foil will help secure the stick in the centre.) Freeze for 1—2 hours until firm.

Meanwhile, put the peaches and the juice into a food processor or blender and process until smooth.

When the raspberry base is firm, pour the peach liquid over the top of the raspberry mixture and freeze for a further 1—2 hours or overnight until firm.

DESSERTS & SWEET TREATS

BANOFFEE PIE

Serves 6–8
Preparation time 15 minutes, plus chilling
Cooking time 10 minutes

250 g (8 oz) **digestive biscuits**, crushed

425 g (14 oz) can **condensed milk**
2 **bananas**

150 ml (1/4 pint) **whipping cream**

Essentials
300 g (10 oz) butter
175 g (6 oz) caster sugar
1 tablespoon lemon juice

Make the crumb case. Melt 125 g (4 oz) butter in a saucepan and stir in the biscuit crumbs. Press the mixture evenly over the base and sides of a deep 20 cm (8 inch) loose-based flan tin. Chill until firm. Make the filling. Put the remaining butter and the sugar in a saucepan and heat gently, stirring, until the butter has melted. Stir in the condensed milk. Bring to the boil, then simmer for 5 minutes, stirring occasionally, until the mixture becomes a caramel colour. Pour into the base and leave to cool, then chill until set.

Slice the bananas and toss them in the lemon juice. Reserve one-quarter of the banana slices for decoration and spread the rest over the filling. Whip the cream until it forms soft peaks and spread it over the top. Decorate with the reserved banana slices.

If liked, sprinkle 25 g (1 oz) grated plain dark chocolate over the top before serving.

LEMON MERINGUE PIE

Serves 6
Preparation time 40 minutes, plus chilling and standing
Cooking time 35—40 minutes

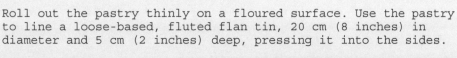

375 g (12 oz) chilled ready-made **sweet shortcrust pastry**
40 g (1½ oz) **cornflour**
grated rind and juice of 2 **lemons**

Essentials
flour, for dusting
200 g (7 oz) caster
  sugar
4 eggs, separated

Roll out the pastry thinly on a floured surface. Use the pastry to line a loose-based, fluted flan tin, 20 cm (8 inches) in diameter and 5 cm (2 inches) deep, pressing it into the sides.

Trim the top and prick the base all over, then chill for 15 minutes. Line with nonstick baking paper, add dry macaroni and bake blind in a preheated oven, 190°C (375°F), Gas Mark 5, for 15 minutes. Remove the paper and macaroni and bake for 5 more minutes. Put 75 g (3 oz) sugar in a bowl with the cornflour and lemon rind, add the egg yolks and mix until smooth.

Make the lemon juice up to 300 ml (½ pint) with water, pour into a saucepan and bring to the boil. Gradually mix into the yolk mixture, whisking until smooth. Pour back into the pan and bring to the boil, whisking until very thick. Pour into the pastry case and spread level.

Whisk the egg whites until they form stiff peaks. Gradually whisk in the remaining sugar, a teaspoonful at a time, then whisk for 1—2 minutes more until thick and glossy. Spoon over the lemon layer to cover and swirl with a spoon. Reduce the oven to 180°C (350°F), Gas Mark 4, and cook for 15—20 minutes until the meringue is golden and cooked through. Leave to stand for 15 minutes before serving.

RHUBARB SLUMPS

Serves 2
Preparation time 10 minutes
Cooking time 20—25 minutes

200 g (7 oz) **rhubarb**, cut into chunks
grated rind and juice of 1/2 **orange**

50 g (2 oz) **oats**

50 ml (2 fl oz) **double cream**

Essentials
50 g (2 oz) caster sugar

Mix together the rhubarb, half the sugar and the orange rind and half the juice in a bowl. Spoon the mixture into 2 individual ramekins.

Put the oats and cream and the remaining sugar and orange juice in a bowl and mix together. Drop spoonfuls of the oat mixture over the surface of the rhubarb mixture.

Set the ramekins on a baking sheet and bake in a preheated oven, 180℃ (350℉), Gas Mark 4, for 20—25 minutes until the topping is browned. Serve hot.

CHOCOLATE BAKED ALASKA

Serves 4—6
Preparation time 10 minutes, plus freezing
Cooking time 5 minutes

1 small, ready-made **sponge flan case**

2 tablespoons **apple juice**

4 tablespoons **cherry, raspberry** or **strawberry jam**

500 ml (17 fl oz) luxury **chocolate ice cream**

Essentials
3 egg whites
125 g (4 oz) caster sugar

Put the flan case in an ovenproof pie dish. Drizzle over the apple juice and spoon the jam evenly over the surface.

Run a blunt knife around the sides of the ice cream to help loosen it from the tub. Upturn the ice cream on top of the flan case. Place the pie dish on a baking sheet and put in the freezer.

Whisk the egg whites in a grease-free bowl until they turn white and thick. Whisk in 1 tablespoon of the sugar at a time until the meringue is smooth, glossy and stiffly peaking.

Use a palette knife to spread the meringue over the prepared ice cream, making sure the ice cream is completely covered and the meringue seals the edge of the flan case. Return to the freezer for at least 1 hour (you can leave it for up to a day).

Bake in a preheated oven, 220°C (425°F), Gas Mark 7, for 5 minutes or until the meringue is just starting to get tinged with brown and serve immediately.

RASPBERRY SHORTBREAD MESS

Serves 2

Preparation time 5 minutes

150 g (5 oz) **raspberries**, roughly chopped

2 **shortbread fingers**, roughly crushed

200 g (7 oz) **fromage frais**

1 tablespoon **icing sugar**

Reserving a few raspberries for decoration, combine all the ingredients in a bowl. Spoon into 2 serving dishes.

Decorate with the reserved raspberries and serve immediately.

PINEAPPLE WITH LIME & CHILLI SYRUP

Serves 4
Preparation time 10 minutes, plus cooling
Cooking time 10 minutes

3 red **chillies**

grated rind and juice of 1 **lime**

1 baby **pineapple**, halved or quartered, cored and cut into wafer-thin slices

Essentials
100 g (3½ oz) caster sugar

Put the sugar in a saucepan with 100 ml (3½ fl oz) water. Heat slowly until the sugar has dissolved, then add the chillies, bring to the boil and boil rapidly until the liquid becomes syrupy. Leave to cool.

Stir the lime rind and juice into the cooled syrup. Lay the pineapple slices on a plate and drizzle the syrup over. Serve chilled with a dollop of ice cream, if liked.

GRILLED PEACHES WITH PASSIONFRUIT

Serves 2
Preparation time 2 minutes
Cooking time 4–5 minutes

4 large ripe **peaches**

1 tablespoon **clear honey**,
plus extra to serve

50 ml (2 fl oz) **Greek yogurt**

pulp from 1 **passionfruit**

Essentials
1 teaspoon ground cinnamon

Cut the peaches in half and discard the stones. Arrange the peach halves, cut side up, in a foil-lined grill pan, drizzle over the honey and dust with the cinnamon.

Cook under a preheated hot grill for 4–5 minutes until lightly charred.

Spoon into serving bowls and serve topped with yogurt, an extra drizzle of honey and the passionfruit pulp.

BERRY WAFFLES

Serves 2
Preparation time 5 minutes
Cooking time 1—2 minutes

125 g (4 oz) **mixed berries**, such as blueberries, blackberries and raspberries

2 **waffles**

2 tablespoons **crème fraîche**

Essentials
15 g (½ oz) butter
15 g (½ oz) caster sugar

Melt the butter in a nonstick frying pan, add the berries and sugar and cook over a high heat, stirring gently, for 1—2 minutes.

Meanwhile, toast or reheat the waffles according to the instructions on the packet. Put a waffle on each serving plate, spoon the berries over the waffles and top each portion with 1 tablespoon crème fraîche. Serve immediately.

APRICOT TARTLETS

Makes 4 tarts
Preparation time 15 minutes
Cooking time 20—25 minutes

375 g (12 oz) ready-rolled **puff pastry** (thawed if frozen)

100 g (3^1/$_2$ oz) **marzipan**

12 canned **apricot halves**, drained

apricot jam, for glazing

Essentials
caster sugar, for sprinkling

Using a saucer as a guide, cut 4 rounds from the pastry, each about 8 cm (3 inches) across. Score a line about 1 cm (½ inch) from the edge of each round with the point of a sharp knife.

Roll out the marzipan to 2.5 mm (⅛ inch) thick and cut out 4 rounds to fit inside the scored circles. Lay the pastry rounds on a baking sheet, place a circle of marzipan in the centre of each and arrange 3 apricot halves, cut side up, on top. Sprinkle a little sugar into each apricot.

Put the baking sheet on top of a second preheated baking sheet and bake in a preheated oven, 200°C (400°F), Gas Mark 6, for 20—25 minutes until the pastry is puffed and browned and the apricots are slightly caramelized around the edges.

While the tarts are still hot brush the tops with apricot jam to glaze. Serve immediately.

QUICK SUMMER PUDDINGS

Serves 2
Preparation time 10 minutes, plus thawing

175 g (6 oz) **mixed berries** (thawed if frozen)

1 tablespoons **vodka** (optional)

4 slices of **white bread**

Essentials
15 g (½ oz) caster sugar

Tip the fruit into a sieve set over a bowl. When the juice has run out, transfer the fruit to a second bowl and mix in the vodka (if used) and the sugar. Use a fluted biscuit cutter to cut circles about 8 cm (3 inches) across from the bread. Dip both sides of 2 pieces of bread into the berry juice, then place them in individual shallow glass serving dishes.

Spoon half the fruit over the bread circles and cover with the remaining bread dipped into the juice. Top with the remaining fruit and juices from the bowl.

Serve with vanilla ice cream, if liked.

STRIPED BERRY SYLLABUBS

Serves 2
Preparation time 15 minutes

150 ml (1/4 pint) **double cream**

finely grated rind of 1/2 **lemon**

75 ml (3 fl oz) **dry cider**

200 g (7 oz) **strawberries**, hulled

Essentials
2½ tablespoons caster sugar

Pour the cream into a bowl, add 1 tablespoon sugar and the lemon rind and whisk until the cream forms soft peaks. Gradually whisk in the cider, then set aside.

Reserve 2 of the smallest strawberries for decoration, then mash the remainder with the remaining sugar.

Spoon one-third of the cream mixture into 2 wine or dessert glasses. Use half the mashed berries to make a thin layer over the cream, then repeat the layers, finishing with a layer of cream. Decorate each glass with a strawberry and chill until required.

CARAMELIZED BANANA PUFF TART

Makes 4 tarts
Preparation time 10 minutes
Cooking time 15—20 minutes

3 **bananas**, sliced

375 g (12 oz) ready-rolled **puff pastry** (thawed if frozen)

3 tablespoons **demerara sugar**

Essentials
1 egg, beaten

Roll the pastry into a 20 cm (8 inch) square and cut the pastry into 4 equal pieces. Place on a baking sheet and use the point of a sharp knife to score a 1 cm (½ inch) border around the edge of each pastry square.

Slice the bananas in half horizontally. Arrange the bananas, cut side up, on the pastry inside the border, then brush the border with the beaten egg. Sprinkle the top of the bananas with the sugar. Bake in a preheated oven, 200°C (400°F), Gas Mark 6, for 15—20 minutes or until the pastry is puffed and golden and the bananas are caramelized.

Serve the tarts hot with whipping cream, if liked.

FREEFORM APPLE TART

Serves 6
Preparation time 10 minutes
Cooking time 20—25 minutes

1 large sheet of **shortcrust pastry**,
   30 cm (12 inch) square (thawed if frozen)

500 g (1 lb) Granny Smith **apples**, peeled,
   cored and thinly sliced

125 g (4 oz) **raisins**

1 tablespoon **icing sugar**, plus extra
   for dusting

Essentials
25 g (1 oz) caster sugar
25 g (1 oz) butter, melted
½ teaspoon ground cinnamon
1 tablespoon milk

Lay the pastry sheet on a baking sheet lined with baking paper and trim each corner to make a roughly round piece of pastry.

Mix together the apples, raisins, caster sugar, melted butter and cinnamon in a bowl until evenly combined. Spoon the apple mixture on to the pastry sheet, arranging it in a circle and leaving a 2.5 cm (1 inch) border. Pull the pastry edges up and over the filling to make a rim. Brush the pastry with the milk and dust with icing sugar.

Bake in a preheated oven, 180°C (350°F), Gas Mark 4, for 20—25 minutes until the pastry is golden and the fruit softened. Dust with icing sugar before serving.

Serve warm with custard, if liked.

RICH CHOCOLATE MOUSSE

Serves 4
Preparation time 5 minutes, plus chilling
Cooking time 3–4 minutes

175 g (6 oz) **plain dark chocolate**, broken into pieces

100 ml (3 fl oz) **double cream**

cocoa powder, for dusting

Essentials
3 eggs, separated

Put the chocolate and cream in a heatproof bowl set over a saucepan of gently simmering water (do not let the bowl touch the water) and stir until the chocolate has melted. Leave to cool for 5 minutes, then beat in the egg yolks one at a time.

Whisk the egg whites in a separate clean bowl until stiff, then lightly fold into the chocolate mixture until combined. Spoon the mousse into 4 dessert glasses or cups and chill for 2 hours. Dust with cocoa powder before serving.

BLUEBERRY & LEMON ICE CREAM

Serves 4
Preparation time 10 minutes, plus freezing

500 g (1 lb) frozen **blueberries**

500 g (1 lb) **Greek yogurt**

125 g (4 oz) **icing sugar**, plus extra to decorate

rind of 2 **lemons**

Essentials
1 tablespoon lemon juice

Reserve a few blueberries for decoration. Put the remainder of the blueberries in a food processor or blender with the yogurt, icing sugar and lemon rind and juice and process until smooth.

Spoon the mixture into a 600 ml (1 pint) freezerproof container and freeze.

Eat when the frozen yogurt is softly frozen and easily spoonable. Before serving, decorate with the reserved blueberries and a sprinkling of icing sugar. Use within 3 days.

SUMMER BERRY SORBET

Serves 2
Preparation time 5 minutes, plus freezing

250 g (8 oz) frozen **mixed summer berries**

75 ml (3 fl oz) **spiced berry cordial**

2 tablespoons **Kirsch** (optional)

1 tablespoon **lime juice**

Put a shallow plastic container in the freezer to chill. Process the frozen berries, cordial, Kirsch (if used) and lime juice in a food processor or blender to a smooth purée. Be careful not to over-process because this will soften the mixture too much.

Spoon into the chilled container and freeze for at least 25 minutes. Spoon into serving bowls and serve.

CARAMEL ICE CREAM CAKE

Serves 8–10
Preparation time 10 minutes, plus standing,
chilling and freezing

1 litre (1 3/4 pints) good-quality **vanilla ice cream**

250 g (8 oz) **digestive biscuits,** crushed

200 g (7 oz) soft **butterscotch fudge**

2 tablespoons **single cream**

Essentials
75 g (3 oz) butter, melted

Take the ice cream from the freezer and leave to stand at room temperature for 30—45 minutes until it has softened.

Meanwhile, put the crushed biscuits in a bowl, add the melted butter and mix together until the biscuits are moistened. Press the biscuit mixture into a 23 cm (9 inch) round springform tin, pressing it up the edge of the tin to give a 2.5 cm (1 inch) side. Chill in the refrigerator for 20 minutes.

Put the fudge and cream in a saucepan and heat gently, stirring, until the fudge has melted.

Carefully spread two-thirds of the fudge mixture over the biscuit case. Spoon the ice cream over the top and level the surface.

Drizzle the remaining caramel over the ice cream with a spoon and freeze for 4 hours. Unmould the cake and serve in wedges.

CHOCOLATE ICE CREAM PIE

Serves 8
Preparation time 15 minutes, plus standing and freezing
Cooking time 5 minutes

500 ml (17 fl oz) good-quality **chocolate ice cream**

200 g (7 oz) plain dark **chocolate digestive biscuits**, broken into coarse crumbs

2 large **bananas**

Essentials
- 75 g (3 oz) butter, plus extra for greasing
- 1 tablespoon lemon juice

Take the ice cream from the freezer and leave to stand at room temperature for 30–45 minutes until it has softened.

Meanwhile, grease and line the base of a 20 cm (8 inch) loose-based fluted flan tin. Melt the butter in a pan. Combine with the biscuit crumbs and press the mixture into the base of the prepared tin.

Slice the bananas, toss in the lemon juice and scatter over the biscuit base.

Spread the ice cream over the bananas, using a palette knife to cover them evenly and smoothly. Freeze for at least 1 hour before serving.

RHUBARB & RASPBERRY CRUMBLE

Serves 4
Preparation time 10 minutes
Cooking time 25 minutes

500 g (1 lb) fresh or frozen **rhubarb**
(thawed if frozen), sliced

125 g (4 oz) fresh or frozen **raspberries**

3 tablespoons **orange juice**

Essentials
200 g (7 oz) plain flour
pinch of salt
150 g (5 oz) butter
200 g (7 oz) caster sugar

Put the flour and salt in a bowl, add the butter
and rub in with the fingertips until the mixture
resembles breadcrumbs. Stir in 150 g (5 oz) sugar.

Mix together the fruits, the remaining sugar and
orange juice and tip into a buttered dish. Sprinkle
over the topping and cook in a preheated oven, 200°C
(400°F), Gas Mark 6, for about 25 minutes or until
golden-brown and bubbling. Remove and serve
immediately.

If liked, serve with raspberry ripple ice cream.

APPLE FRITTERS

Serves 4
Preparation time 15 minutes
Cooking time about 10 minutes

4 **dessert apples**, cored and thickly sliced

150 g (5 oz) frozen **blackberries**

icing sugar, for dusting

Essentials
2 eggs
125 g (4 oz) plain flour
4 tablespoons caster sugar
150 ml (¼ pint) milk
vegetable oil, for deep-
    frying

Separate one egg and put the white into one bowl and the
yolk and the whole egg into a second bowl. Add the flour
and half the caster sugar to the second bowl. Whisk the
egg white until if forms soft peaks, then use the same
whisk to beat the flour mixture until smooth, gradually
whisking in the milk. Fold in the egg white.

Pour the oil into a deep, heavy-based saucepan until
it comes one-third of the way up the side. Heat the
oil to 180—190°C (350—375°F) or until a cube of bread
browns in 30 seconds.

Dip a few apple slices into the batter and turn
gently to coat. Lift out one slice at a time and lower
carefully into the oil. Deep-fry, in batches, for
2—3 minutes, turning until evenly golden. Remove
with a slotted spoon and drain on kitchen paper.

Meanwhile, put the blackberries, remaining sugar and
2 tablespoons water in a small saucepan and heat for
2—3 minutes until hot. Arrange the fritters on serving
plates, spoon the blackberry sauce around and dust with
a little icing sugar.

SULTANA & GINGER RICE PUDDING

Serves 4
Preparation time 15 minutes
Cooking time about 2 hours

65 g (2½ oz) **pudding rice**

30 g (1¼ oz) **sultanas**

15 g (½ oz) ready-chopped **candied ginger**

finely grated rind of ½ **lemon**

Essentials
2 tablespoons caster sugar
600 ml (1 pint) milk
25 g (½ oz) butter
grated nutmeg, to sprinkle

Put the rice, sugar, sultanas, ginger and lemon rind into a shallow 1.2 litre (2 pint) ovenproof dish. Pour the cold milk over the top and mix the ingredients together.

Cut the butter into tiny pieces and dot over the top of the milk. Sprinkle with a little nutmeg and cook in a preheated oven, 150°C (300°F), Gas Mark 2, for 2 hours or until the top is golden-brown, the rice is tender and the milk is thick and creamy. Serve warm.

CARAMELiZED ORANGE & PiNEAPPLE

Serves 4
Preparation time 10 minutes
Cooking time 10 minutes

4 oranges
1 small pineapple

Essentials
175 g (6 oz) caster sugar

Remove the rind from 2 of the oranges and cut it into fine strips. Place the rind in a saucepan of boiling water and simmer for 2 minutes. Remove and drain well.

Put the sugar and 125 ml (4 fl oz) water into a saucepan and heat gently, swishing the pan constantly until the sugar has dissolved. Increase the heat and boil the syrup until it turns golden-brown. Take care not to overcook the caramel: if it gets too dark, carefully add 2 tablespoons water. (Stand back when you add water because the caramel will spit.) Set aside when ready.

Cut a slice off the top and bottom of each orange. Set the orange on one of these cut sides and take a knife around the side of the orange, cutting away the skin and pith. Cut across the orange into 6—7 slices.

Skin and core the pineapple, taking care to remove the 'eyes' close to the skin. Cut the pineapple into quarters and then into slices.

Arrange the fruit in alternating layers in a heatproof dish. Sprinkle over the orange rind, pour over the caramel and leave to stand until required.

CHOCOLATE NEMESIS & BLUEBERRIES

Serves 12
Preparation time 20 minutes, plus cooling
Cooking time about 1 hour

325 g (11 oz) **plain dark chocolate,**
  chopped

300 g (10 oz) **blueberries**

Essentials
225 g (7½ oz) caster sugar
225 g (7½ oz) butter, diced,
  plus extra for greasing
5 eggs

Lightly grease a 23 cm (9 inch) springform cake tin and line it with nonstick baking paper.

Gently heat 150 g (5 oz) sugar in a pan with 100 ml (3½ fl oz) water until it has dissolved into a light syrup. Remove from the heat.

Melt the chocolate with the butter in a bowl over a pan of simmering water. Pour the hot syrup into the melted chocolate. Remove from the heat.

Whisk the remaining sugar with the eggs until they are light and foamy and tripled in volume. Slowly beat the chocolate into the whisked eggs until well combined.

Tip the mixture into the prepared tin and stand the tin on a trivet in a roasting tin. Three-quarters fill the roasting tin with boiling water and bake in a preheated oven, 120°C (250°F), Gas Mark ½, for 50 minutes until just firm.

Leave the cake to cool in the tin in the water. Serve in wedges with the blueberries.

WARM CHOCOLATE FROMAGE FRAIS

Serves 6
Preparation time 1 minute
Cooking time 4 minutes

300 g (10 oz) **plain dark chocolate**

500 ml (17 fl oz) **fromage frais**

1 teaspoon **vanilla extract**

Melt the chocolate in a bowl over a pan of simmering water. Remove from the heat.

Add the fromage frais and vanilla extract and quickly stir together.

Spoon the mixture into 6 little pots or dessert glasses and serve immediately.

CAKES
& BAKES

VANILLA CUPCAKES

Makes 12 cakes
Preparation time 15 minutes
Cooking time 20 minutes

2 teaspoons **vanilla extract**

250 g (8 oz) **icing sugar**

Essentials

300 g (10 oz) butter, softened

150 g (5 oz) caster sugar

175 g (6 oz) self-raising flour

3 eggs

Line a 12-section bun tray with paper or foil cake cases or stand 12 silicone cases on a baking sheet. Put 150 g (5 oz) butter and the caster sugar, flour, eggs and 1 teaspoon vanilla extract in a bowl and beat together until light and creamy.

Spoon the mixture into the cake cases and bake in a preheated oven, 180°C (350°F), Gas Mark 4, for 20 minutes or until risen and just firm to the touch. Transfer to a wire rack to cool.

Put the remaining butter and the icing sugar in a bowl and beat well with a wooden spoon until smooth and creamy. Mix in the remaining vanilla extract and 2 tablespoons hot water and beat again. Use the buttercream to top the cold cupcakes.

CHILLI CHOCOLATE CHIP MUFFINS

Makes 8 muffins
Preparation time 10 minutes
Cooking time 20 minutes

50 g (2 oz) **cocoa powder**

1 teaspoon **baking powder**

150 g (5 oz) soft **light brown sugar**

125 g (4 oz) **chilli chocolate**, chopped, or **plain dark chocolate** and a pinch of **chilli powder**

Essentials
200 g (7 oz) self-raising flour
1 egg, lightly beaten
250 ml (8 fl oz) milk
50 g (2 oz) butter, melted
vegetable oil, for brushing

Cut a 15 cm (6 inch) square from baking paper and use it as a template to cut 7 more squares. Fold them all into quarters, open them out flat and set aside.

Sift the flour, cocoa powder and baking powder into a bowl and stir in the sugar. Beat together the egg, milk and melted butter in a small bowl, then mix into the dry ingredients until just combined (don't over-mix). Fold in the chocolate.

Lightly brush each square of baking paper with oil and press each piece into the hole of a muffin tray. Spoon the chocolate mixture into the lined holes and bake in a preheated oven, 200°C (400°F), Gas Mark 6, for 20 minutes until risen and golden. Leave to cool slightly on a wire rack and serve warm.

CHOCOLATE REFRIGERATOR CAKE

Makes 30 fingers
Preparation time 15 minutes, plus chilling
Cooking time 5 minutes

500 g (1 lb) **plain dark chocolate**, chopped

100 g (3¹/2 oz) **digestive biscuits**, roughly crushed

125 g (4 oz) **dried figs**, roughly chopped

100 g (4 oz) **hazelnuts**, toasted and roughly chopped

Essentials
125 g (4 oz) butter, plus extra for greasing

Grease a 17 x 23 cm (7 x 9 inch) rectangular cake tin and line the base with nonstick baking paper. Put the chocolate and butter in a heatproof bowl set over a saucepan of gently simmering water (don't let the bowl touch the water) and stir over a low heat until melted. Stir in all the remaining ingredients. Spoon the mixture into the prepared tin. Press well into the base and sides of the tin and smooth the surface with a palette knife.

Cover with foil and chill for 4 hours or overnight in the refrigerator. Carefully work round the edges of the cake with the palette knife and unmould on to a board, removing the paper from the base. Serve in thin fingers.

MINI CHOCOLATE MERINGUES

Makes 6 meringues
Preparation time 15 minutes
Cooking time 1¼ hours

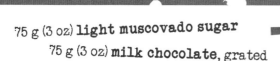

75 g (3 oz) **light muscovado sugar**

75 g (3 oz) **milk chocolate**, grated

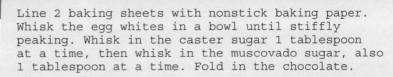

Essentials
3 egg whites
75 g (3 oz) caster sugar

Line 2 baking sheets with nonstick baking paper. Whisk the egg whites in a bowl until stiffly peaking. Whisk in the caster sugar 1 tablespoon at a time, then whisk in the muscovado sugar, also 1 tablespoon at a time. Fold in the chocolate.

Drop teaspoonfuls of the meringue mixture on to the baking sheets. Bake in a preheated oven, 140°C (275°F), Gas Mark 1, for 1¼ hours, then turn off the heat and leave in the oven for another 30 minutes.

The meringues go well with strawberries and cream.

ORANGE & SULTANA SCONES

Makes 10 scones
Preparation time 20 minutes
Cooking time 10-12 minutes

75 g (3 oz) **sultanas**
grated rind of 1 **orange**

Essentials
375 g (12 oz) self-raising
  flour
50 g (2 oz) butter, diced
50 g (2 oz) caster sugar,
  plus extra for sprinkling
1 egg, beaten
150—200 ml (5—7 fl oz) milk

Put the flour in a mixing bowl or a food processor. Add the butter and rub in with your fingertips or process until the mixture resembles fine breadcrumbs. Stir in the sugar, sultanas and orange rind. Add all but 1 tablespoon of the egg, then gradually mix in enough of the milk to make a soft but not sticky dough.

Knead lightly, then roll out on a lightly floured surface until 1.5 cm (¾ inch) thick. Stamp out 5.5 cm (2¼ inch) circles using a plain round biscuit cutter. (Don't be tempted to roll out the dough thinner and make more scones because they will just look mean and miserly.) Transfer to a lightly greased baking sheet. Re-knead the trimmings and continue rolling and stamping out until you have made 10 scones.

Brush the tops with the reserved egg and sprinkle lightly with a little extra sugar. Bake in a preheated oven, 200°C (400°F), Gas Mark 6, for 10—12 minutes until well risen and the tops are golden. Leave to cool on the baking sheet.

Serve the scones warm or just cold, split and filled with jam and clotted cream, if liked. They are best eaten on the day they are made.

HAZELNUT & BLUEBERRY CAKES

Makes 12 cakes
Preparation time 20 minutes
Cooking time 20 minutes

150 ml (1/4 pint) **crème fraîche**

50 g (2 oz) finely **ground hazelnuts**

1 1/2 teaspoons **baking powder**

125 g (4 oz) fresh **blueberries**

Essentials
3 eggs
150 g (5 oz) caster sugar
175 g (6 oz) plain flour

Line a 12-section bun tray with paper or foil cake cases or stand 12 silicone cases on a baking sheet. Put the eggs, crème fraîche and sugar in a mixing bowl and whisk together until smooth.

Add the ground hazelnuts, flour and baking powder and mix together.

Spoon the mixture into the cake cases and arrange the blueberries evenly on them, pressing them lightly into the mixture. Bake in a preheated oven, 180°C (350°F), Gas Mark 4, for about 20 minutes until well risen and golden.

These are best eaten on the day they are made.

LEMON & ORANGE DRIZZLE CAKES

Makes 12 cakes
Preparation time 20 minutes
Cooking time 12—15 minutes

grated rind and juice of 1 **lemon**

grated rind and juice of 1 **orange**

Essentials
250 g (8 oz) self-raising flour
200 g (7 oz) caster sugar
3 eggs
2 tablespoons milk
100 g (3½ oz) butter, melted

Line a 12-section bun tray with paper or foil cake cases or stand 12 silicone cases on a baking sheet. Put the flour in a mixing bowl, add half the sugar and half the lemon and orange rind. Lightly beat the eggs and milk together, then add to the bowl with the melted butter. Beat together until just smooth. Spoon the mixture into the cake cases and bake in a preheated oven, 190°C (375°F), Gas Mark 5, for 12—15 minutes until well risen and the tops are craggy and firm to the touch.

Meanwhile, make the lemon and orange syrup. Put the remaining sugar and grated citrus rind in a bowl. Strain in the fruit juices, then mix together until the sugar has just dissolved.

As soon as the cakes come out of the oven, loosen the edges and turn out. Arrange in a shallow dish, prick the tops with a fine skewer or fork and drizzle the syrup over, little by little, until absorbed by the cakes. Leave to cool. The cakes are best served on the day they are made.

REAL CHOCOLATE BROWNIES

Makes 10 brownies
Preparation time 15 minutes, plus cooling
Cooking time 30 minutes

75 g (3 oz) **plain dark chocolate**, chopped

1/2 teaspoon **baking powder**

Essentials
75 g (3 oz) butter, plus extra
  for greasing
2 eggs
250 g (8 oz) caster sugar
100 g (3½ oz) plain flour

Grease a 20 cm (8 inch) square tin and line the base with nonstick baking paper.

Melt the chocolate with the butter in a bowl set over a pan of simmering water.

Whisk together the eggs and sugar in a bowl until the mixture is pale and creamy. Stir the melted chocolate into the egg mixture. Sieve in the flour and baking powder and fold together.

Turn the mixture into the prepared tin and bake in a preheated oven, 190°C (375°F), Gas Mark 5, for 25 minutes until the brownies are firm on top and a skewer inserted into the centre comes out clean. Leave to cool in the tin for 5 minutes, then cut into squares.

EASY COCONUT & CHOCOLATE CAKES

Makes 6 cakes
Preparation time 20 minutes, plus cooling
Cooking time 30 minutes

75 g (3 oz) sweetened **shredded tenderized coconut**

1 teaspoon **baking powder**

200 g (7 oz) **milk chocolate**, chopped

Essentials
175 g (6 oz) butter, melted, plus extra for greasing
175 g (6 oz) self-raising flour
175 g (6 oz) caster sugar
3 large eggs, lightly beaten

Grease and line the base of 8 heart-shaped moulds, each about 5 cm (2 inch) in diameter.

Reserving one-third, put the coconut in a large bowl. Add the flour, baking powder, sugar, eggs and melted butter. Mix together well until smooth. Spoon the mixture into the moulds and bake in a preheated oven, 180°C (350°F), Gas Mark 4, for 20 minutes until the cakes are risen and a skewer inserted into the centre comes out clean. Turn on to a wire rack to cool, placing the rack over a baking sheet.

Melt the chocolate in a bowl over a pan of simmering water. Use a palette knife to spread the chocolate around the sides of the cakes, then pour the rest of the chocolate over the top of the cakes, allowing it to trickle down the sides. Sprinkle over the reserved coconut to decorate and allow to set before serving.

EASY CHOCOLATE FUDGE CAKE

Serves 12
Preparation time 10 minutes, plus cooling
Cooking time 50—55 minutes

425 g (14 oz) **plain dark chocolate,** chopped
150 ml (1/4 pint) **single cream**

Essentials
250 g (8 oz) butter, plus extra for greasing
4 eggs, beaten
125 g (4 oz) caster sugar
225 g (7½ oz) self-raising flour, sifted

Grease a 20 x 30 cm (8 x 12 inch) baking tin and line the base with baking paper.

Put 250 g (8 oz) chocolate and the butter in a heatproof bowl set over a saucepan of gently simmering water (don't let the bowl touch the water) and stir over a low heat until melted. Leave to cool for 5 minutes.

Meanwhile, using an electric hand-held whisk, whisk together the eggs and sugar in a bowl for 5 minutes until thick. Beat in the cooled chocolate mixture and fold in the flour.

Spoon the mixture into the prepared tin and bake in a preheated oven, 160°C (325°F), Gas Mark 3, for 45—50 minutes until risen and firm to the touch. Leave to cool in the tin for 10 minutes, then turn out on to a wire rack to cool completely, removing the paper from the base.

Meanwhile, make the icing. Put the remaining chocolate in a saucepan with the cream and heat gently, stirring, until the chocolate has melted. Leave to cool for 1 hour until thickened to a pouring consistency, then spread over the cake. Leave to set for 30 minutes before serving.

APRICOT & ORANGE SWISS ROLL

Serves 8
Preparation time 30 minutes
Cooking time 18—20 minutes

200 g (7 oz) ready-to-eat **dried apricots**

200 ml (7 fl oz) **apple juice**

grated rind of 1 **orange**

Essentials
4 eggs
125 g (4 oz) caster sugar,
  plus extra for sprinkling
125 g (4 oz) plain flour,
  sifted

Line a 30 x 23 cm (12 x 9 inch) roasting or a swiss roll tin
with nonstick baking paper.

Simmer the apricots and apple juice in a saucepan, covered,
for 10 minutes or until most of the liquid has been absorbed.
Purée, then leave to cool.

Put the eggs, sugar and orange rind in a large heatproof bowl
set over a saucepan of gently simmering water. Whisk, using an
electric hand-held whisk, for 5—10 minutes until thick and foamy
and the whisk leaves a trail when lifted above the mixture.

Gently fold in the sifted flour. Pour the mixture into the
prepared tin and ease into the corners. Bake in a preheated
oven, 200°C (400°F), Gas Mark 6, for 8—10 minutes until the
sponge is golden-brown and begins to shrink away from the sides
and the top springs back when gently pressed with a fingertip.

Meanwhile, cover a clean damp tea towel with nonstick baking
paper and sprinkle with sugar. Quickly turn out the cooked
sponge on to the paper. Carefully peel off the lining paper.
Spread the apricot purée over the sponge, then, starting with
a short side, roll up to form a log. Leave to cool and serve.

CLASSIC SHORTBREAD

Makes 16 biscuits
Preparation time 15 minutes, plus chilling
Cooking time 18—20 minutes

125 g (4 oz) **rice flour**

Essentials
250 g (8 oz) butter, at
  room temperature
125 g (4 oz) caster sugar,
  plus extra for sprinkling
250 g (8 oz) plain flour
pinch of salt

Beat together the butter and sugar in a mixing bowl
or a food processor until pale and creamy. Sift in
the flour, rice flour and salt and mix or process
briefly until the ingredients just come together.
Transfer to a work surface and knead lightly to form
a soft dough. Shape into a disc, wrap in clingfilm
and chill for 30 minutes.

Divide the dough in half and roll out each piece on
a lightly floured surface to a 20 cm (8 inch) round.
Transfer to 2 ungreased baking sheets. Score each
round with a sharp knife, marking it into 8 equal
wedges, prick with a fork and use your fingers to
flute the edges.

Sprinkle over a little sugar and bake in a preheated
oven, 190°C (375°F), Gas Mark 5, for 18—20 minutes
until golden. Remove from the oven and, while still
hot, cut into wedges through the score marks. Leave
to cool on the baking sheet for 5 minutes, then
transfer to a wire rack to cool. Store in an
airtight tin.

CHOCOLATE CHIP COOKIES

Makes 16 cookies
Preparation time 10 minutes, plus cooling
Cooking time 15 minutes

175 g (6 oz) soft light brown sugar
1 teaspoon vanilla extract
1 teaspoon baking powder
250 g (8 oz) plain dark chocolate chips

Essentials
125 g (4 oz) butter, diced
  and softened
1 egg, lightly beaten
1 tablespoon milk
200 g (7 oz) plain flour

Line a large baking sheet with nonstick baking paper.

In a large bowl beat together the butter and sugar until light and fluffy. Mix in the vanilla extract, then gradually beat in the egg, beating well after each addition. Stir in the milk.

Sift the flour and baking powder into a separate large bowl, then fold into the butter and egg mixture. Stir in the chocolate chips.

Drop level tablespoonfuls of the mixture on to the prepared baking sheet, leaving about 3.5 cm (1½ inches) between each cookie, then lightly press with a floured fork. Bake in a preheated oven, 180°C (350°F), Gas Mark 4, for 15 minutes or until lightly golden. Transfer to a wire rack to cool.

LEMON COOKIES

Makes 18—20 cookies
Preparation time 15 minutes, plus cooling
Cooking time 15—20 minutes

2 teaspoons grated **lemon rind**

100 g (3½ oz) coarse **cornmeal**

icing sugar, for dusting

Essentials

125 g (4 oz) butter, diced
and softened
125 g (4 oz) caster sugar
2 egg yolks
150 g (5 oz) plain flour

Line a baking sheet with nonstick baking paper.
In a bowl beat together the butter and sugar until
light and fluffy. Mix in the egg yolks, lemon rind,
flour and cornmeal until a soft dough forms.

Roll out the dough on a lightly floured surface to
1 cm (½ inch) thick. Use a 6 cm (2½ inch) round
cutter to cut out rounds from the dough, re-rolling
the trimmings.

Transfer to the prepared baking sheet and bake in
a preheated oven, 160°C (325°F), Gas Mark 3, for
15—20 minutes or until lightly golden. Transfer to
a wire rack to cool, then dust with icing sugar.

CHUNKY CHERRY FUDGE COOKIES

Makes 18 cookies
Preparation time 15 minutes
Cooking time 10—12 minutes

75 g (3 oz) **light muscovado sugar**
1 teaspoon **vanilla extract**
100 g (3 1/2 oz) or 4 **chocolate-covered fudge bars**, chopped
75 g (3 oz) **glacè cherries**, roughly chopped

Essentials
75 g (3 oz) butter, softened
75 g (3 oz) caster sugar
1 egg, beaten
175 g (6 oz) self-raising flour

Line 2 baking sheets with nonstick baking paper.
Put the butter, both sugars and vanilla extract in a mixing bowl and beat together until pale and creamy. Stir in the egg and flour and mix until smooth. Stir in the fudge and cherries, then spoon 18 mounds on to the baking sheets, leaving space between for them to spread during cooking.

Bake in a preheated oven, 180°C (350°F), Gas Mark 4, for 10—12 minutes until golden-brown. Leave to harden for 1—2 minutes, then loosen and transfer to a wire rack to cool completely. These are best eaten on the day they are made.

PEANUT BUTTER COOKIES

Makes 32 cookies
Preparation time 10 minutes
Cooking time 12 minutes

150 g (5 oz) soft **brown sugar**

125 g (4 oz) **chunky peanut butter**

1/2 teaspoon **baking powder**

125 g (4 oz) **unsalted peanuts**

Essentials
vegetable oil, for greasing
125 g (4 oz) butter, softened
1 egg, lightly beaten
150 g (5 oz) plain flour

Lightly oil 3 large baking sheets.

Beat together the butter and sugar in a mixing bowl or a food processor until pale and creamy. Add the peanut butter, egg, flour and baking powder and stir together until combined. Stir in the peanuts.

Drop large teaspoonfuls of the mixture on to the baking sheets, leaving 5 cm (2 inch) space between for them to spread during cooking.

Flatten the mounds slightly with a fork and bake in a preheated oven, 190°C (375°F), Gas Mark 5, for 12 minutes until golden around the edges. Leave to cool on the baking sheets for 2 minutes, then transfer to a wire rack to cool completely.

VANILLA & COCOA BISCUITS

Makes 18 biscuits
Preparation time 15 minutes, plus chilling and cooling
Cooking time 10-12 minutes

1 teaspoon **vanilla extract**

1 tablespoon **cocoa powder**

125 g (4 oz) **icing sugar**

Essentials
125 g (4 oz) butter, softened
125 g (4 oz) caster sugar
175 g (6 oz) plain flour
1 large egg
1 egg yolk

Blend together the butter, caster sugar and vanilla extract in a mixing bowl or food processor. Add the flour, cocoa powder, whole egg and yolk. Blend again until the mixture forms a ball. Knead the dough lightly until it is smooth. Wrap in clingfilm and chill for 30 minutes. Roll out the dough between 2 sheets of nonstick baking paper until it is 2.5 mm (⅛ inch) thick. Cut out 15 hearts using a 5 cm (2 inch) cutter. Reroll the trimmings and cut out 3 more heart shapes. Leave the hearts on the baking paper and slide the paper on to 2 baking sheets.

Bake in a preheated oven, 180°C (350°F), Gas Mark 4, for 10—12 minutes or until the biscuits are firm and golden. Cool for 5 minutes, then transfer to a wire rack to cool completely.

Make the icing. Sift the icing sugar into a bowl, add 1 tablespoon cold water, stir and add another 1 tablespoon water to make a smooth piping consistency. Transfer to a piping bag with a fine plain nozzle and pipe various designs around the edges of the cookies or drizzle over with a teaspoon.

FRUITY FLAPJACKS

Makes 12 flapjacks
Preparation time 20 minutes
Cooking time 25—30 minutes

150 g (5 oz) **golden syrup**
450 g (14 1/2 oz) **rolled oats**
75 g (3 oz) **light muscovado sugar**
125 g (4 oz) **mixed dried fruit**, such as cranberries, sour cherries, blueberries

Essentials
vegetable oil, for greasing
200 g (7 oz) butter

Lightly grease a 23 cm (9 inch) square and 6 cm (2½ inch) deep tin.

Melt the butter and golden syrup in a pan over a low heat. Remove from the heat and mix in the oats, sugar and fruit. Stir everything together.

Turn the mixture into the prepared tin and press down with the back of a spoon. Bake in a preheated oven, 190°C (375°F), Gas Mark 5, for 25—30 minutes until golden and firm. Cool. Cut into 12 slices.

TOFFEE RICE CRISPY RINGS

Makes 10 biscuits
Preparation time 10 minutes
Cooking time 5 minutes

150 g (5 oz) **chewy toffees**
2 tablespoons **cocoa powder**
200 g (7 oz) **marshmallows**
175 g (6 oz) **rice crispies**

Essentials
vegetable oil, for greasing
50 g (2 oz) butter

Lightly grease a 10 cm (4 inch) ring (rum baba) mould.

Melt the toffees with the cocoa powder and butter in a nonstick pan over a gentle heat. Stir the mixture with a wooden spoon, then tip in the marshmallows (there is no need to stir again at this stage). Return the pan to the heat for 1 minute, then stir quickly to mix. Add one-third of the rice crispies and mix them into the toffee mixture. Add the rest of the rice crispies in 2 batches, stirring well after each addition.

Take a handful of the rice crispie mixture and press it into the mould to make a ring shape. Press it down firmly with the palm of your hand, then twist and upturn it to release it from the mould. Place it on a sheet of nonstick baking paper. Repeat with the rest of the mixture to make 10 rings in all. Allow to set before serving.

CORNFLAKE CRUNCHIES

Makes 20 cakes
Preparation time 15 minutes, plus chilling
Cooking time 5 minutes

200 g (7 oz) **plain dark chocolate**, chopped

3 tablespoons **golden syrup**

125 g (4 oz) **cornflakes**

mini marshmallows, sliced, to decorate

Essentials
50 g (2 oz) butter

Arrange 20 paper or foil cake cases or silicone cases on a muffin or baking sheet.

Put the chocolate in a saucepan with the butter and golden syrup. Heat gently, stirring occasionally, until the chocolate and butter have completely melted and the mixture is smooth and glossy. Stir in the cornflakes and mix until completely coated in the chocolate.

Spoon the cornflake mixture into the cake cases and chill for 2–3 hours until firm. Decorate with sliced mini marshmallows.

INDEX

A

all-in-one veggie breakfast 24
apples: apple fritters 223
  freeform apple tart 216
  pork steaks with apples 56
  tropical juice 164
apricots: apricot and orange
  Swiss roll 240
  apricot tartlets 212
Asian chicken parcels 144
Asian citrus chicken skewers
  174
asparagus: baked vegetable
  frittata 114
aubergines: aubergine and
  mozzarella bake 109
  aubergine and mozzarella
  panini 199
  aubergine dip 189
  chickpea tagine 173
avocados: prawn, mango and
  avocado salad 177

B

bacon: bacon and eggs 22
  bacon and maple syrup
  pancakes 32
  macaroni cheese with bacon
  90
  potato and bacon cakes 30
  spaghetti carbonara 73
baked Alaska, chocolate 207
baked beans: quick sausage and
  bean casserole 50
balsamic vinegar 16
bamboo chicken with cashews
  136
bamboo shoots: vegetables in
  yellow bean sauce 135
bananas: banana and peanut
  butter smoothie 39
  banoffee pie 204
  caramelized banana puff tart
  215

chargrilled fruit with
  chilli salt 169
chocolate banana croissants
  35
chocolate ice cream pie 221
banoffee pie 204
basil pesto 74
beans: caldo verde 172
  chilli con carne 59
  mini beef and bean burgers
  184
  mixed bean kedgeree 107
  quick sausage and bean
  casserole 50
beef: beef goulash 51
  beef with black bean sauce
  130
  Bolognese sauce 75
  chilli con carne 59
  mini beef and bean burgers
  184
  steak and ale casserole 63
  steak with horseradish 55
  Thai chilli beef burgers 188
beetroot and berry smoothie
  163
berry waffles 211
biscuits: chocolate chip
  cookies 242
  chunky cherry fudge cookies
  244
  classic shortbread 241
  lemon cookies 243
  peanut butter cookies 245
  toffee rice crispy rings 248
  vanilla and cocoa biscuits
  246
black bean sauce, beef with
  130
blackberries: apple fritters
  223
blueberries: beetroot and
  berry smoothie 163
  blueberry and lemon ice
  cream 218
  chocolate nemesis and
  blueberries 226
  hazelnut and blueberry cakes
  235
  mixed berry salad 168
  sugared fruit pancakes 33
Bolognese sauce 75
bread: aubergine and
  mozzarella panini 199

boiled eggs with mustard
  soldiers 20
bread and butter pudding 65
brunch croque monsieur 196
chocolate and cinnamon eggy
  bread 37
easy fish pie 53
pastrami with red onion
  chutney 197
quick summer puddings 213
seared chicken sandwich 187
tuna, pesto and mozzarella
  ciabatta 198
see also pizza; toast
brioche sandwich, chocolate 36
broccoli: broccoli and sausage
  pasta 82
  vegetables in yellow bean
  sauce 135
brownies, real chocolate 237
brunch croque monsieur 196
bucatini, pancetta and tomato
  83
bulgar wheat: Lebanese lentil
  and bulgar salad 176
burgers: mini beef and bean
  184
  potato and cheese 185
  Thai chilli beef 188
butter 17
butter bean and tomato
  casserole 118
butterscotch: caramel ice
  cream cake 220

C

cabbage: caldo verde 172
Caesar salad 178
cakes: apricot and orange
  Swiss roll 240
  caramel ice cream cake 220
  chocolate refrigerator cake
  232
  easy chocolate fudge cake
  239
  easy coconut and chocolate
  cakes 238
  hazelnut and blueberry cakes
  235
  lemon and orange drizzle
  cakes 236
  real chocolate brownies 237
  vanilla cupcakes 230

victoria sponge 68
caldo verde 172
cannellini beans: caldo verde 172
caramel: caramel ice cream cake 220
  caramelized banana puff tart 215
  caramelized orange and pineapple 225
carrots: carrot and ginger soup 171
  curried carrot and lentil soup 46
  roast root vegetable soup 48
cashews, bamboo chicken with 136
casseroles: beef goulash 51
  butter bean and tomato casserole 118
  chickpea and tomato casserole 111
  chickpea tagine 173
  lamb hotpot 156
  quick sausage and bean casserole 50
  steak and ale casserole 63
cauliflower: potato and cauliflower curry 110
chapattis: tuna enchiladas 158
cheese: aubergine and mozzarella bake 109
  aubergine and mozzarella panini 199
  baked cheese fondue 159
  brunch croque monsieur 196
  cheese and tomato omelette 28
  cheesy pasta and mushroom bake 91
  chicken stacks 152
  chicken with spring herbs 143
  classic tomato pizza 92
  creamy blue cheese pasta 77
  dolcelatte and spinach gnocchi 145
  easy-cook tomato spaghetti 76
  macaroni cheese with bacon 90
  mushroom and spinach lasagne 89

onion and mushroom quesadillas 102
pastrami with red onion chutney 197
pesto turkey kebabs 148
pizza bianchi 96
potato and cheese burgers 185
potato gratin 108
red pepper and cheese tortellini 78
scrambled eggs with goats' cheese and herbs 26
spaghetti carbonara 73
spinach and ricotta pitta bread pizza 98
spinach, feta and egg tarts 120
three-cheese pizza 94
tomato, tapenade and feta tart 115
tortilla pizza with salami 95
tuna and pineapple pizza 93
tuna fish cakes 186
tuna, pesto and mozzarella ciabatta 198
cherry fudge cookies 244
chicken: Asian chicken parcels 144
Asian citrus chicken skewers 174
bamboo chicken with cashews 136
chicken and hummus wraps 190
chicken and rice bake 58
chicken satay 193
chicken stacks 152
chicken tacos 192
chicken with spring herbs 143
coconut chicken 126
crispy spiced chicken wings 134
devilled chicken 151
fast chicken curry 125
feel-good broth 43
jerk chicken wings 191
lemon chilli chicken 154
lightly spiced chicken nuggets 183
lime, ginger and coriander chicken 153

rice noodles with lemon chicken 129
roast chicken with lemon 146
seared chicken sandwich 187
sesame chicken katzu 139
spicy chicken naan bread pizzas 99
tandoori chicken 127
teriyaki chicken 128
chickpeas: chickpea and tomato casserole 111
  chickpea tagine 173
  chunky chickpea and pasta soup 45
chilli: Asian chicken parcels 144
  chargrilled fruit with chilli salt 169
  chickpea and tomato casserole 111
  chilli chocolate chip muffins 231
  chilli con carne 59
  chilli powder 15
  chilli sauce 16
  lemon chilli chicken 154
  pasta with garlic, oil and chilli 87
  pineapple with lime and chilli syrup 209
  stir-fried hoisin beans 138
Chinese fried rice 137
chips: fish 'n' oven chips 57
  healthy spiced chips 195
chocolate: chilli chocolate chip muffins 231
  chocolate and cinnamon eggy bread 37
  chocolate baked Alaska 207
  chocolate banana croissants 35
  chocolate brioche sandwich 36
  chocolate chip cookies 242
  chocolate fondue 66
  chocolate ice cream pie 221
  chocolate nemesis and blueberries 226
  chocolate overload 67
  chocolate refrigerator cake 232
  chunky cherry fudge cookies 244
  cornflake crunchies 249

easy chocolate fudge cake 239
easy coconut and chocolate cakes 238
frothy hot chocolate 69
mini chocolate meringues 233
real chocolate brownies 237
rich chocolate mousse 217
toffee and chocolate popcorn 200
vanilla and cocoa biscuits 246
warm chocolate fromage frais 227
chorizo carbonara 81
cider: striped berry syllabubs 214
coconut and chocolate cakes 238
coconut chicken 126
condensed milk: banoffee pie 204
cookies: chocolate chip 242
chunky cherry fudge 244
lemon 243
peanut butter 245
cornflake crunchies 249
courgette and herb risotto 105
cream: fettuccine all'Alfredo 88
rhubarb slumps 206
striped berry syllabubs 214
croissants: chocolate banana 35
spiced citrus 34
croque monsieur, brunch 196
crumble, rhubarb and raspberry 222
cupcakes, vanilla 230
curries: curried carrot and lentil soup 46
curried red lentils 117
curry paste 16
fast chicken curry 125
potato and cauliflower curry 110
smoked mackerel kedgeree 175
Thai chilli beef burgers 188
Thai green pork curry 124
Thai red pork and bean curry 133
custard: rhubarb and custard smoothie 38

D
devilled chicken 151
dip, aubergine 189
dolcelatte and spinach gnocchi 145
dried fruit: fruity flapjacks 247
drinks: banana and peanut butter smoothie 39
beetroot and berry smoothie 163
frothy hot chocolate 69
rhubarb and custard smoothie 38
tropical juice 164

E
easy fish pie 53
eggs 17
all-in-one veggie breakfast 4
bacon and eggs 22
baked vegetable frittata 114
boiled eggs with mustard soldiers 20
cheese and tomato omelette 8
chocolate and cinnamon eggy bread 37
chorizo carbonara 81
eggs Benedict 23
pea and leek omelette 121
pesto scrambled eggs 27
potato rösti with frazzled eggs 29
rösti with ham and eggs 31
scrambled eggs with goats' cheese and herbs 26
spaghetti carbonara 73
spinach, feta and egg tarts 120
sweetcorn and pepper frittata 119
enchiladas, tuna 158
equipment 13
exotic fruit salad 165

F
feel-good broth 43
fettuccine al'Alfredo 88
figs: chocolate refrigerator cake 232
fig and honey pots 167
finger-licking garlic prawns 157
fish: easy fish pie 53
fish 'n' oven chips 57
see also haddock, tuna etc
flapjacks, fruity 247
flour 14
fondue: baked cheese 159
chocolate 66
freeform apple tart 216
French beans: stir-fried hoisin beans 138
Thai red pork and bean curry 133
French bread pizzas with salami 97
French onion soup 49
French toast 21
frittata: baked vegetable 114
sweetcorn and pepper 119
fritters, apple 223
fromage frais, warm chocolate 227
fruit 11
berry waffles 211
chargrilled fruit with chilli salt 169
exotic fruit salad 165
quick summer puddings 213
summer berry sorbet 219
see also apples, strawberries etc
fruity flapjacks 247
fudge: chunky cherry fudge cookies 244
easy chocolate fudge cake 239

G
garlic 17
creamy garlic mussels 147
finger-licking garlic prawns 157
lemon chilli chicken 154
roast chicken with lemon 146
ginger: carrot and ginger soup 171
sultana and ginger rice pudding 224
gnocchi: dolcelatte and spinach gnocchi 145
gnocchi with sage butter 112

goats' cheese, scrambled eggs with herbs and 26
goulash, beef 51
grapefruit: spiced citrus croissants 34
gratin, potato 108

H

haddock: fish 'n' oven chips 57
ham: brunch croque monsieur 196
eggs Benedict 23
rösti with ham and eggs 31
hazelnuts: chocolate refrigerator cake 232
hazelnut and blueberry cakes 235
herbs 15
hoisin beans, stir-fried 138
hollandaise sauce 23
honey: fig and honey pots 167
horseradish, steak with 55
hotpot, lamb 156
hummus: chicken and hummus wraps 190
hygiene 12

I J K

ice cream: blueberry and lemon ice cream 218
caramel ice cream cake 220
chocolate baked Alaska 207
chocolate ice cream pie 221
chocolate overload 67
ingredients 14—17
jerk chicken wings 191
kebabs: Asian citrus chicken skewers 174
chicken satay 193
minted lamb skewers 149
pesto turkey kebabs 148
kedgeree: mixed bean 107
smoked mackerel 175
kiwifruit: pear, kiwifruit and lime juice 162

L

lamb: lamb hotpot 156
minted lamb skewers 149
shepherd's pie 52
tasty teatime pasties 61

lasagne, mushroom and spinach 89
Lebanese lentil and bulgar salad 176
leeks: baked vegetable frittata 114
leek and potato soup 42
pea and leek omelette 121
tomato and leek rice 106
lemon 17
blueberry and lemon ice cream 218
lemon and orange drizzle cakes 236
lemon chilli chicken 154
lemon cookies 243
lemon meringue pie 205
roast chicken with lemon 146
lentils: curried carrot and lentil soup 46
curried red lentils 117
Lebanese lentil and bulgar salad 176
lettuce: Caesar salad 178
lime: lime, ginger and coriander chicken 153
pear, kiwifruit and lime juice 162
pineapple with lime and chilli syrup 209
lollies, multicoloured fresh fruit 201

M

macaroni cheese with bacon 90
mackerel: smoked mackerel kedgeree 175
mangoes: chargrilled fruit with chilli salt 169
prawn, mango and avocado salad 177
tropical juice 164
margarine 17
marshmallows: toffee rice crispy rings 248
marzipan: apricot tartlets 212
mayonnaise: potato salad 179
meat: hygiene 12
see also *beef, pork etc*
meatballs: sausage meatballs, peas and pasta 79
meringue: chocolate baked Alaska 207

lemon meringue pie 205
mini chocolate meringues 233
strawberry crush 166
minted lamb skewers 149
minted pea soup 44
mixed berry salad 168
Moroccan grilled sardines 150
mousse, rich chocolate 217
muffins: chilli chocolate chip muffins 231
eggs Benedict 23
mushrooms: all-in-one veggie breakfast 24
cheesy pasta and mushroom bake 91
lamb hotpot 156
mixed mushrooms on toast 25
mushroom and spinach lasagne 89
mushroom soup 47
mushroom stroganoff 62
onion and mushroom quesadillas 102
wild mushroom pappardelle 86
mussels, creamy garlic 147

N

naan breads: minted lamb skewers 149
spicy chicken naan bread pizzas 99
noodles with lemon chicken 129

O

oats: fruity flapjacks 247
rhubarb slumps 206
oils 15—16
olive oil 15
olives: spicy tuna, tomato and olive pasta 85
omelettes: cheese and tomato 28
pea and leek 121
onions: French onion soup 49
onion and mushroom quesadillas 102
pastrami with red onion chutney 197
sausage and sweet potato hash 60
oranges: apricot and orange Swiss roll 240

caramelized orange and pineapple 225
lemon and orange drizzle cakes 236
orange and sultana scones 234

PQ

pak choi, sesame prawns with 131
pancakes: bacon and maple syrup 32
sugared fruit 33
pancetta and tomato bucatini 83
panini, aubergine and mozzarella 199
pappardelle, wild mushroom 86
Parma ham: pesto turkey kebabs 148
parsnips: roast root vegetable soup 48
passionfruit: exotic fruit salad 165
grilled peaches with passionfruit 210
tropical juice 164
pasta: Bolognese sauce 75
broccoli and sausage pasta 82
cheesy pasta and mushroom bake 91
chorizo carbonara 81
chunky chickpea and pasta soup 45
classic basil pesto 74
creamy blue cheese pasta 77
easy-cook tomato spaghetti 76
feel-good broth 43
fettuccine all'Alfredo 88
macaroni cheese with bacon 90
mushroom and spinach lasagne 89
pancetta and tomato bucatini 83
pasta with garlic, oil and chilli 87
penne with sausage and tomato 84
quick tomato pasta sauce 72

red pepper and cheese tortellini 78
sausage meatballs, peas and pasta 79
spaghetti carbonara 73
spicy tuna, tomato and olive pasta 85
tuna Niçoise spaghetti 80
wild mushroom pappardelle 86
pasties, tasty teatime 61
pastrami with red onion chutney 197
peaches: grilled peaches with passionfruit 210
multicoloured fresh fruit lollies 201
peanut butter: banana and peanut butter smoothie 39
chicken satay 193
peanut butter cookies 245
pear, kiwifruit and lime juice 162
peas: minted pea soup 44
pea and leek omelette 121
risi e bisi 103
sausage meatballs, peas and pasta 79
summer green pea soup 170
penne: cheesy pasta and mushroom bake 91
chorizo carbonara 81
penne with sausage and tomato 84
spicy tuna, tomato and olive pasta 85
peppers: beef goulash 51
red pepper and cheese tortellini 78
roasted stuffed peppers 113
sweetcorn and pepper frittata 119
teriyaki chicken 128
pesto: classic basil pesto 74
pesto scrambled eggs 27
pesto turkey kebabs 148
tuna, pesto and mozzarella ciabatta 198
pies: shepherd's pie 52
tasty teatime pasties 61
pineapple: caramelized orange and pineapple 225
chargrilled fruit with chilli salt 169

exotic fruit salad 165
pineapple with lime and chilli syrup 209
tuna and pineapple pizza 93
pizza: classic tomato pizza 92
French bread pizzas with salami 97
pizza bianchi 96
spicy chicken naan bread pizzas 99
spinach and ricotta pitta bread pizza 98
three-cheese pizza 94
tortilla pizza with salami 95
tuna and pineapple pizza 93
polenta with herbs 116
pollock, deep-fried 155
popcorn, toffee and chocolate 200
pork: pork steaks with apples 56
Thai green pork curry 124
Thai red pork and bean curry 133
potatoes: all-in-one veggie breakfast 24
fish 'n' oven chips 57
gnocchi with sage butter 112
healthy spiced chips 195
lamb hotpot 156
leek and potato soup 42
pea and leek omelette 121
potato and bacon cakes 30
potato and cauliflower curry 110
potato and cheese burgers 185
potato gratin 108
potato rösti with frazzled eggs 29
potato salad 179
potato wedges 182
roast chicken with lemon 146
rösti with ham and eggs 31
shepherd's pie 52
poultry, hygiene 12
prawns: Chinese fried rice 137
finger-licking garlic prawns 157
prawn, mango and avocado salad 177
sesame prawns with pak choi 131

prosciutto: chicken stacks
152
  pizza bianchi 96
quesadillas, onion and
  mushroom 102

R

raspberries: beetroot and
  berry smoothie 163
  multicoloured fresh fruit
  lollies 201
  raspberry shortbread mess
  208
  rhubarb and raspberry
  crumble 222
red kidney beans: chilli con
  carne 59
  mini beef and bean burgers
  184
red pepper and cheese
  tortellini 78
refrigerator cake, chocolate
  232
rhubarb: rhubarb and custard
  smoothie 38
  rhubarb and raspberry
  crumble 222
  rhubarb slumps 206
rice: chicken and rice bake
  58
  Chinese fried rice 137
  courgette and herb risotto
  105
  mixed bean kedgeree 107
  risi e bisi 103
  smoked mackerel kedgeree
  175
  spinach and lemon risotto
  104
  sultana and ginger rice
  pudding 224
  tomato and leek rice 106
rice crispy rings, toffee
  248
rice noodles with lemon
  chicken 129
risi e bisi 103
risotto: courgette and herb
  105
  spinach and lemon 104
rösti: potato rösti with
  frazzled eggs 29
  rösti with ham and eggs 31

S

sage butter, gnocchi with 112
salads: Caesar salad 178
  Lebanese lentil and bulgar
  salad 176
  potato salad 179
  prawn, mango and avocado
  salad 177
salami: French bread pizzas
  with salami 97
  tortilla pizza with salami
  95
salmon, tea-smoked 132
salt 14
  chargrilled fruit with
  chilli salt 169
sandwich, seared chicken 187
sardines, Moroccan grilled 150
satay, chicken 193
sauces: Bolognese 75
  hollandaise 23
  quick tomato pasta 72
sausages: Bolognese sauce 75
  broccoli and sausage pasta
  82
  chorizo carbonara 81
  penne with sausage and
  tomato 84
  quick sausage and bean
  casserole 50
  sausage and sweet potato
  hash 60
  sausage meatballs, peas and
  pasta 79
  sausages and mustard mash
  142
  toad in the hole 54
scones, orange and sultana 234
sesame chicken katzu 139
sesame prawns with pak choi
  131
shepherd's pie 52
shortbread: classic shortbread
  241
  raspberry shortbread mess
  208
smoked mackerel kedgeree 175
smoothies: banana and peanut
  butter 39
  beetroot and berry 163
  rhubarb and custard 38
sorbet, summer berry 219
soups: caldo verde 172
  carrot and ginger soup 171

chunky chickpea and pasta
  soup 45
curried carrot and lentil
  soup 46
feel-good broth 43
French onion soup 49
leek and potato soup 42
minted pea soup 44
mushroom soup 47
roast root vegetable soup 48
summer green pea soup 170
soy sauce 16
spaghetti: classic basil pesto
  74
  easy-cook tomato spaghetti
  76
  pasta with garlic, oil and
  chilli 87
  spaghetti carbonara 73
  tuna Niçoise spaghetti 80
spices 15
spinach: dolcelatte and
  spinach gnocchi 145
  mushroom and spinach lasagne
  89
  spinach and lemon risotto
  104
  spinach and ricotta pitta
  bread pizza 98
  spinach, feta and egg tarts
  120
sponge, victoria 68
steak and ale casserole 63
steak with horseradish 55
sticky toffee puddings 64
stock cubes 14
strawberries: chocolate fondue
  66
  mixed berry salad 168
  strawberry crush 166
  striped berry syllabubs 214
stroganoff, mushroom 62
sugared fruit pancakes 33
sultanas: orange and sultana
  scones 234
  sultana and ginger rice
  pudding 224
summer berry sorbet 219
summer green pea soup 170
summer puddings, quick 213
sunflower oil 16
sweet chilli sauce 16
sweet potatoes: baked sweet
  potatoes 194

potato wedges 182
sausage and sweet potato
hash 60
sausages and mustard mash
142
sweetcorn and pepper frittata
119
Swiss roll, apricot and orange
240
syllabub, striped berry 214

T

tacos, chicken 192
tagine, chickpea 173
tandoori chicken 127
tapenade: tomato, tapenade and
feta tart 115
tarts: apricot tartlets 212
caramelized banana puff tart
215
freeform apple tart 216
spinach, feta and egg tarts
120
tomato, tapenade and feta
tart 115
tea-smoked salmon 132
teatime pasties 61
teriyaki chicken 128
Thai chilli beef burgers 188
Thai green pork curry 124
Thai red pork and bean curry
133
three-cheese pizza 94
toad in the hole 54
toast: French 21
mixed mushrooms on 25
pesto scrambled eggs 27
scrambled eggs with goats'
cheese and herbs 26

toffee: banoffee pie 204
sticky toffee puddings 64
toffee and chocolate popcorn
200
toffee rice crispy rings 248
tomato purée 16
tomatoes: all-in-one veggie
breakfast 24
bacon and eggs 22
Bolognese sauce 75
butter bean and tomato
casserole 118
cheese and tomato omelette
28
chickpea and tomato
casserole 111
chilli con carne 59
classic tomato pizza 92
curried red lentils 117
easy-cook tomato spaghetti
76
fast chicken curry 125
pancetta and tomato bucatini
83
penne with sausage and
tomato 84
quick sausage and bean
casserole 50
quick tomato pasta sauce 72
roasted stuffed peppers 113
spicy tuna, tomato and olive
pasta 85
tomato and leek rice 106
tomato, tapenade and feta
tart 115
tortellini, red pepper and
cheese 78
tortillas: aubergine dip 189
chicken and hummus wraps
190

onion and mushroom
quesadillas 102
tortilla pizza with salami
95
tropical juice 164
tuna: spicy tuna, tomato and
olive pasta 85
tuna and pineapple pizza 93
tuna enchiladas 158
tuna fish cakes 186
tuna Niçoise spaghetti 80
tuna, pesto and mozzarella
ciabatta 198
turkey: pesto turkey kebabs
148

V W Y

vanilla and cocoa biscuits
246
vanilla cupcakes 230
vegetable oil 16
vegetables 11
roast root vegetable soup 48
vegetables in yellow bean
sauce 135
see also peas, tomatoes etc
victoria sponge 68
vinegar, balsamic 16
waffles, berry 211
wild mushroom pappardelle 86
wraps, chicken and hummus 190
yellow bean sauce, vegetables
in 135
yogurt: blueberry and lemon
ice cream 218
fig and honey pots 167
strawberry crush 166

Acknowledgements

Executive Editor Eleanor Maxfield
Senior Editor Charlotte Macey
Deputy Creative Director Karen Sawyer
Designer Balley Design
Production Controller Linda Parry